AIR CAMPAIGN

HO CHI MINH TRAIL 1964–73

Steel Tiger, *Barrel Roll*, and the secret air wars in Vietnam and Laos

PETER E. DAVIES | ILLUSTRATED BY ADAM TOOBY

OSPREY PUBLISHING
Bloomsbury Publishing Plc
Kemp House, Chawley Park, Oxford OX2 9PH, UK
1385 Broadway, 5th Floor, New York, NY 10018, USA
29 Earlsfort Terrace, Dublin 2, Ireland
Email: info@ospreypublishing.com

OSPREY is a trademark of Osprey Publishing

First published in Great Britain in 2020

A catalog record for this book is available from the British Library.

ISBN: PB 9781472842534; eBook 9781472842541;
ePDF 9781472842510; XML 9781472842527

21 22 23 24 25   10 9 8 7 6 5 4 3 2

Maps by www.bounford.com
Diagrams by Adam Tooby
3D BEVs by Paul Kime
Index by Alan Rutter
Typeset by PDQ Digital Media Solutions, Bungay, UK
Printed and bound in India by Replika Press Private Ltd.

Osprey Publishing supports the Woodland Trust, the UK's leading woodland
conservation charity.

To find out more about our authors and books visit www.ospreypublishing.com.
Here you will find extracts, author interviews, details of forthcoming events,
and the option to sign up for our newsletter.

Glossary

AAA	antiaircraft artillery
ABCCC	Airborne Command and Control Center
ACS/W	Air Commando Squadron/Wing
ARRS	Air Rescue and Recovery Squadron
ARVN	Army of the Republic of Vietnam
BDA	bomb damage assessment
CAS	close air support
CBU	cluster bomb unit
DMZ	demilitarized zone
ECM	electronic countermeasures
FAC	forward air controller
ISC	Infiltration Surveillance Center
LGB	laser-guided bomb
LORAN	long-range radio navigation system
LS	Lima Site (airfield)
LZ	landing zone
MACV-SOG	Military Assistance Command, Vietnam – Studies and Observations Group
MACV	Military Assistance Command, Vietnam
MAG	Marine Aircraft Group
NVA	North Vietnamese Army
RESCAP	Rescue Combat Air Patrol
ROE	rules of engagement
RS/W	Reconnaissance Squadron/Wing
RTAFB	Royal Thai Air Force Base
SAR	search and rescue
SAWD	Special Air Warfare Detachment
SOS	Special Operations Squadron
SOW	Special Operations Wing
SRS/W	Strategic Reconnaissance Squadron/Wing
SW	Strategic Wing
TACAN	tactical air navigation
TASS	Tactical Air Support Squadron
TAW	Tactical Airlift Wing
TCW	Troop Carrier Wing
TDY	temporary duty
TEWS	Tactical Electronic Warfare Squadron
TFS/W	Tactical Fighter Squadron/Wing
TRS/W	Tactical Reconnaissance Squadron/Wing
VAL	US Navy Light Attack Squadron
VC	Vietnamese Communists (Viet Cong)
VNAF	[South] Vietnamese Air Force
VPAF	[North] Vietnamese People's Air Force

CONTENTS

INTRODUCTION

Although its surviving sections have become profitable long-distance footpaths for adventurous tourists visiting Laos, the Ho Chi Minh Trail during the Vietnam War was the scene of heroic effort, extreme hardship, and loss of life for the Vietnamese, Laotians, and the many US servicemen who strived to carry out their government's policy of attempting to close the Trail down. For over 15 years, it was North Vietnam's main conduit for troops and supplies for its military units, operating in South Vietnam to overthrow the Saigon government and unite the country under Hanoi's leadership.

In 1965, American maps showed the Trail as a skeletal arrangement of narrow forest trails used by local tribes, combined with some dry-season roads that still remained from previous French colonial occupation. Within nine years, it became a complex network of all-weather roads, bypasses, tracks, bridges, and fuel pipelines stretching for thousands of miles.

Additional weapons for the insurgents in the South were transported from China in smugglers' trawlers off Vietnam to secret coastal locations, and by sea from North Vietnam to Cambodia, where Chinese and Soviet ships could unload for onward carriage by land along the Sihanouk Trail, established in May 1966. The sea route, which carried 14 percent of the cargo in 1969, was more efficient than human porters and trucks on the Trail, but more vulnerable to US seaborne interdiction. The Trail network through Laos provided the most direct route from the North, albeit through almost impenetrable primeval forest in many places. After the loss of Cambodian ports in 1970, the Trail in Laos was expanded to accommodate the extra traffic.

The network remained open throughout the war despite a monumental, frustrating US effort to disrupt it. Much of that effort was directed at an area of the Laotian "panhandle," which extended for 125 miles from the demilitarized zone (DMZ) in the east to the Thai border, with the "base complex area 604" around the small town of Tchepone as its trailhead. Underground, a vast tunnel network was constructed. In the Cu Chi tunnel complex, subterranean passages up to five levels deep were begun in 1948 and extended over 150 miles from the Cambodian border to the edges of Saigon. They included hospitals, command and control centers, and living accommodation.

Climate and topography of the area became major factors for both sides. Severe monsoon weather made travel extremely difficult but shielded its travelers from air attack. From May to October, tracks, often only 2ft wide, became deep in mud or blocked by overflowing streams while low-lying areas were flooded. Most traffic was moved in the dryer period from mid-October to March. Extreme mountainous terrain such as the steep Truong Son Range and dense triple-canopy jungle necessitated extraordinary ingenuity and endurance by the porters, each carrying up to 60lb of cargo. It also necessitated hazardous tactics by US aircrew attempting to intercept the traffic. Over four million tons of US ordnance were expended on the Trail but a large proportion of the million tons of supplies and around two million troops and workers traveling those routes still completed the journey.

Initially, those personnel were 700 South Vietnamese who had moved to the North following the division of the country in 1954, when French colonial rule had ended. They returned to the South armed with captured French weapons, to become the core of the Viet Cong ("Vietnamese Communists") force in the first stage in the North's planned invasion. As the war expanded, they were supplemented or replaced by regular North Vietnamese soldiers. By June 1968, there were over a hundred North Vietnamese Army (NVA) infantry battalions in the South, far outnumbering Viet Cong forces.

Most trail tracks, diversions, and bypasses were passable only on foot. Porters often pushed French or Soviet bicycles laden with up to 200lb of supplies. (US Army)

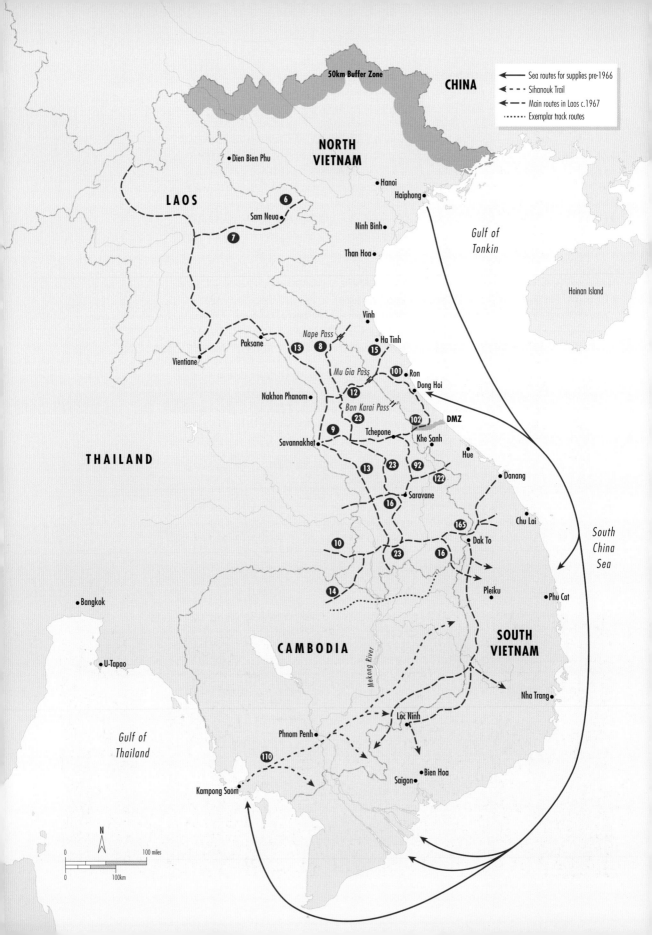

OPPOSITE THE MAIN ROUTES ON THE HO CHI MINH TRAILS, *c.*1967

Group 559

Unification of North and South Vietnam, finally achieved after Hanoi's invasion of the South in April 1975, was planned from mid-1959 with arrangements to supply Viet Cong and North Vietnamese forces in the South. A basic component of the plan was the establishment of a Trail network by Transportation Group 559, overseen by Col Vo Bam and later by Lt Gen Dong Si Nguyen. This organization was divided into geographical administrative units called Binh Trams. They remained at work throughout the war, employing over 100,000 workers (many of them Chinese, or Laotian slave laborers) to maintain and defend roads, bridges, tracks, and supply dumps along the tortuous routes which eventually ran for over 12,000 miles, mostly in Laos. It began on North Vietnam's roads and fragmented into many tracks and footpaths, as well as paved roads, as it extended into Laos, eventually meeting the Sihanouk Trail in Cambodia. At many points it crossed into South Vietnam and some sections passed through the DMZ. Prior to 1970, many Group 559 engineers returned north during the monsoon season when substantial building work was impossible.

Infiltration movements were organized in June 1959 and by 1963 over 40,000 insurgents and their weapons had traveled south. Slow, laborious transport by porters had to be supplemented by trucks to carry the required quantities of supplies despite the greater risk of air attack. In 1965, Transportation Group 559 (renamed the Truong Son Army in 1970) began to lay all-weather paved roads where possible at the rate of 280 miles per year, rising to 650 miles by 1971. Road-building equipment could then be moved to areas where further 18ft-wide hard surfaces and bridges were constructed. US pilots began to see captured American bulldozers and graders at work on sections of the Trails.

From 1966, large quantities of Soviet and Chinese infantry and artillery weapons were supplied to the North. Many of the small arms were taken south by the NVA troops and kept there, but the ammunition (including 122mm rockets) had to be laboriously hand carried. The Trail also became a route for injured troops or the families of Viet Cong to be evacuated to the North. Its more secure, sheltered sections in Laos and Cambodia became rear areas for the NVA forces in the South, including command and control centers, maintenance for military equipment, ammunition stockpiles, and truck parks. In 1970, a support area

Ammunition often comprised around 90 percent of trail cargo. Porters, many of them female students, knew that the few shells that they had carried for over three months would be fired off in a few seconds by troops in Laos. (Van Bang/AFP via Getty Images)

covering two square miles and housing 182 storage bunkers, 18 mess halls, and training facilities was uncovered in Cambodia. All had been transported along the Trails. A similarly extensive supply complex was revealed near Tchepone during Operation *Lam Son 719* by the South Vietnamese Army in 1971. In addition to its eight base camps, three hospitals, 20 truck parks, and voluminous storage bunkers, it was defended by 59 antiaircraft guns and three SA-2 ground-to-air missile sites.

Network development also required way stations at one-day intervals of travel, camouflaged vehicle parks, and storage areas. Up to a third of the Trails were camouflaged with netting and foliage. Underground bunkers and medical facilities were established for travelers to feed and rest. Once the convoys had reached South Vietnam, food could often be acquired locally. A major expansion began in 1964 after the initial supply routes were fortuitously discovered by the South Vietnamese. At that early stage, the weakness and confusion in the Saigon government persuaded Hanoi that an invasion of the South might be feasible.

By 1975, General Giap felt that the Trail network was finally complete. The North had built over 3,000 miles of fuel pipelines to supply its vehicles. The pipeline did not reach Laos until 1968 so fuel was carried in plastic containers until then. Pumps to keep the fuel flow moving had to be hidden underground to disguise their radiant heat from airborne infrared sensors. After the withdrawal of US troops in 1972, the main arteries of the Trail from Tchepone towards Saigon included 650 miles of 25ft-wide paved highway which greatly facilitated the North's ultimate invasion of South Vietnam in 1975.

Washington's response

Nominally an independent state after 1954 and neutral as a result of the 1962 Geneva Accords between the USA, Russia, and North Vietnam, Laos occupied a key "buffer" position in Southeast Asia between China, Vietnam, Cambodia, Thailand, and Burma. Like Vietnam, it had experienced centuries of conflict and invasion, but in US eyes its neutrality was vital in containing Communist ambitions. After 1954, civil war broke out between Laotian government forces (supported by France and the USA) and the Communist Pathet Lao, sponsored by North Vietnam. By 1961, North Vietnam had deployed thousands of troops into Laos to support the Pathet Lao, but also to pave the way for the Ho Chi Minh Trail, or Truong Son Road. Although North Vietnam signed the Accords, it quickly became apparent that it had no intention of honoring them. Its continued incursions into Laos were conducted covertly and the secret construction of the Trail network through Laos became a primary focus for Hanoi.

A weak Laotian government did little to resist and the USA could not provide open military opposition to what was clearly a North Vietnamese Army (NVA) invasion. The International Control Commission, appointed to oversee neutrality, could not monitor NVA activity. The air war over northern Laos, Operation *Barrel Roll*, was therefore conducted secretly in support of General Vang Pao's Hmong guerrillas and the Royal Laotian Army in deterring Pathet Lao and North Vietnamese incursions. America officially continued to observe the Geneva Accords and the very influential US Ambassador in Laos, William H. Sullivan, who was given power to enforce this policy by President John F. Kennedy, was energetic in opposing any US military ground action to counter North Vietnamese interference and in preventing the basing of US aircraft in Laos, apart from a handful of CIA-controlled light planes. However, the USA sponsored and supplied a guerrilla army of up to 30,000 Laotians from local tribes, mainly the Hmong, under secret CIA management, with Air America and other civilian contractors as its covert aerial transport and counter-insurgency arm.

A covert air campaign therefore became the only feasible way of tackling the Trail problem. By March 1964, General William C. Westmoreland, commander of the Military Assistance Command, Vietnam (MACV), realized the importance of the Ho Chi Minh Trail and wanted a quick solution by using four Army divisions to seal off the infiltration routes through the DMZ and into Laos. His philosophy, derived from his World War II experience as an artilleryman, was to use massive force to try and crush an enemy in the shortest time. However, the US focus was on defending South Vietnam from within South Vietnam, and President Johnson stated that he would not "widen the war." Inevitably, these pre-conditions precluded the use of soldiers to install any sort of troop-controlled barrier across the Trail, but it also facilitated Hanoi's task in proceeding with its infiltration project. The use of short-range radars such as the AN/PPS-4 portable unit which could detect vehicles or people at three miles' range and protect US firebases, or the PS-33A sound detector, was ruled out.

During the Korean War, the Fifth Air Force commander, Lt Gen Earle E. Partridge, commented that "the paramount deficiency of the USAF as regards air-ground operations is our inability to seek out and destroy the enemy at night." That situation persisted in 1964 in an air force which was still fixated on its nuclear deterrent role, but operations in Southeast Asia against an enemy who moved mainly at night had to continue with the USAF's predominantly day-fighting tactical assets, while better solutions were researched.

In 1961, four RF-101Cs made daylight reconnaissance flights over Laos that produced mosaic photo coverage of the Trail routes and strongholds. Additional "Able Mable" RF-101Cs arrived at Don Mueang, Thailand, later in 1961, joined by two "Black Watch" B-26s for night photo reconnaissance and two "Patricia Lynn" RB-57Es with infrared scanners. All these reconnaissance types apart from the RF-4C Phantom (which arrived in October 1965) suffered from inadequate navigation equipment for night operations. The Geneva Accords ruled out reconnaissance flights over Laos from November 1962 to May 1964, although U-2s provided some covert, high-altitude imagery.

From 1964, in *Barrel Roll* strikes supporting Vang Pao, F-105D Thunderchiefs of the 36th Tactical Fighter Squadron (TFS) deployed to Korat RTAFB (Royal Thai Air Force Base), Thailand on August 12, 1964, and two days later they hit Pathet Lao antiaircraft artillery (AAA) positions on the Plain of Jars, which had shot down an AT-28 Trojan. Four aircraft made repeated strafing attacks on a 37mm gun site, but Lt David Graben's F-105D (62-4371) was so badly damaged that it was written off on its return. *Barrel Roll* strikes in Laos by 18th TFW F-105Ds began on December 15, 1964. They located targets for Laotian T-28D Trojans, supplied in 1962 by the CIA in the Class A program for use against the Pathet Lao. Their pilots were trained by the USAF's 56th Special Operations Wing (SOW) under

Two 562nd TFS F-105Ds over Laos, late in 1965, with M117 bombs and 2.75in rockets. *Barrel Roll* strikes in Laos by 18th TFW F-105Ds began on December 15, 1964, and F-105Ds escorted RF-101C reconnaissance flights over Laos. Thunderchiefs flew trail missions throughout most of the war. (USAF)

Maj Harry Aderholt at Udorn RTAFB from 1964, with Thai and Laotian pilots receiving secret training under Operation *Waterpump*. Similar training of South Vietnamese pilots had begun in *Farm Gate* in November 1961 at Bien Hoa airbase AB.

At Udorn in May 1966, volunteer US pilots were also trained. They were "sheep dipped" by removing any military identities in order to make them "plausibly deniable," and flew unmarked O-1 Bird Dogs, U-6 Beavers, T-28 "Tangos," and Helio Couriers, wearing civilian clothes. They flew forward air control (FAC, initially "FAG": forward air guide) missions for airstrikes and interdiction under Laotian control and the authority of the CIA and US Ambassador. They operated from several primitive Lima Site (LS) airstrips including the 600×50ft "airfield" at LS 85 on Phou Pha Thi mountain, the location of a top-secret radar system that assisted *Rolling Thunder* strikes over North Vietnam. When the site was attacked by hand-grenade dropping North Vietnamese An-2 Colt biplanes in January 1967, an Air America UH-1 helicopter gave chase and shot down at least one of the intruders with an Uzi submachine gun. The site was captured by the NVA in March 1968.

Southern Laos

In the panhandle area of southern Laos, Operation *Steel Tiger* was organized to interdict the sections of the Trail that led from North Vietnam into Laos, South Vietnam, and Cambodia through four main channels; the Keo Neua, Mu Gia, Ban Karai, and Ban Laboy Passes. To the north, the Plain of Jars contained supply routes from North Vietnam on Chinese-built roads from Dien Bien Phu across the northern part of Laos. It also contained the heavily defended Barthelemy Pass.

The Laotian government saw no benefit in attempting to intervene in this area, as the communist threat seemed to be directed at South Vietnam rather than Laos. They regarded the region around Tchepone as essentially North Vietnamese and not worth defending. Also, Pathet Lao aggression in Laos increased whenever the Laotian government appeared to be supporting increased US attacks on Trail targets. This in turn diverted US air assets to defend the Laotian Army.

By 1969, there were nine battalions of irregular Lao troops with 4,000 men, operating covertly in small teams but relying on air support. They formed road-watch teams to observe and report on Trails movement, for which they were inserted and recovered by helicopter, but the North Vietnamese sometimes captured teams and used them as bait to attack the recovery helicopters. Douglas A-1 Skyraiders were provided as escorts to attack these ambushes.

As the conflict intensified, President Johnson authorized airstrikes on the Laotian sections of the Ho Chi Minh Trail. The Trails area was demarcated to facilitate the organization of air attacks, and the most active area was the *Steel Tiger* zone, divided into northern (*Cricket*) and southern (*Tiger Hound* from December 1965) sections. Attacks on traffic there began with a night mission by B-57Bs supported by C-130 flare-droppers on April 3, 1965. Volunteer "Raven" pilots in small observation aircraft, exercising a considerable degree of personal initiative, began to direct strikes over the *Tiger Hound* area in 1966. Special forces from the Military Assistance Command, Vietnam – Studies and Observations Group (MACV-SOG)

were inserted into the jungle in extremely hazardous conditions from October 18, 1965, to find targets. In one of those early ventures, a large supply depot was successfully attacked in 88 sorties by strike aircraft. The Ravens' proximity to enemy defenses was emphasized by their discarding of their armored helmets so that they could hear gunfire around them more clearly.

Cricket missions, under FAC by Ravens or CIA-sponsored Air America (whose motto was: "Fly the Friendly Skies of Southeast Asia") pilots, began in January 1966. The first official airstrike on a Trail target took place on December 14, 1964, when four F-105D Thunderchiefs attacked a bridge near Nape. Thunderchiefs continued to fly missions over the Trail throughout most of the war years, but the truck-busting task proved to be challenging. *Steel Tiger* results for July–September 1966 indicated that it took an average of six F-105 sorties to destroy each truck. On good days, an attack could blow away cover revealing more trucks and resulting in a chain of secondary explosions. A July 1966 mission uncovered and destroyed a 100-ton ammunition dump 200ft long and 10ft high. The success rate was not helped by a standing rule of engagement forbidding attacks on vehicles that were more than 200 yards from the road. Given adequate warning, the drivers could often find diversionary tracks or shelter to take them to safety.

When the *Tiger Hound* program began in December 1965, F-105Ds operated with Nakhon Phanom-based 505th Tactical Control Group O-1E Bird Dog FACs, flying 809 sorties against Trail targets that month. Their more productive missions resulted in the destruction of whole convoys, but success was often limited by the delays in gaining permission for a strike via the arcane command structure in Vientiane, Laos. This could take up to a week. From May 1966, F-105s flew *Gate Guard* night missions with "Blind Bat" C-130 or B-66 flare-droppers, but Ubon-based 497th TFS "Night Owl" F-4C Phantom IIs and 606th SOS "Nimrod" A-26Ks increasingly took those missions. The A-26Ks' accuracy and endurance were particularly valued by FACs. At that time, around 80 percent of bombing missions in central Laos were conducted by these F-105s, F-4Cs, and A-26Ks, and losses rose. Twenty F-105s and 13 F-4Cs were lost over Laos by February 1968.

The consequences of ejecting over most areas of the country were grim, as F-105 pilot Col Jack Broughton admitted. "We all knew that if we had to punch out over Laos we would be at the mercy of brutal people and that we could expect inhumane torture at best. Fear of capture was the worst fear we knew." His assistant deputy strike leader Hal Bingaman recalled having to try and identify the remains of a 354th TFS F-105 pilot who had bailed out over northern Laos. "He had been found hanging in a tree, still in his parachute, stripped naked and flayed of his skin."

After the refusal of Westmoreland's demand for four Army divisions, at least three plans were drawn up to use US forces to cut off and patrol the network in Laos, or to improve the roads running across Laos to Thailand so that troops could be emplaced to intercept traffic. The capture of the Tchepone supply hub was included in much of the planning. However, Westmoreland's main brief was to tackle the Viet Cong in South Vietnam, and President Johnson resisted open military involvement in neutral Laos to cut the Trails.

Instead, Washington embarked upon Operation *Rolling Thunder*, a bombing campaign against North Vietnam which was intended to deter Hanoi from its longstanding ambitions in the South. Punctuated by frequent pauses to assess their effect on Hanoi's morale and by highly restrictive rules of engagement that precluded decisive results, these attacks wrought considerable destruction but failed to soften the North's resolve or affect the growth of the Trails network. Unlike the USA, Hanoi had no scruples about conducting military operations in a neutral country, but activity by CIA-sponsored units in Laos remained secret. The use of airbases in neutral Thailand would be harder to disguise.

Scientific solutions

Instead of direct military intervention in Laos, various alternative means of strangling the North's supply chain were suggested. In January 1966, Professor Roger Fisher from Harvard Law School suggested a 660ft-deep barrier of barbed wire fences, sensors, and landmines stretching for 160 miles along the south of the DMZ and into Laos to stop the traffic en route to the Trails network and isolate it for air attack. Radar and surveillance posts would have monitored those Project *Dye Marker* "McNamara Line" fences. Although Admiral Ulysses S. Grant Sharp Jr, Commander-in-Chief in the Pacific, estimated that this project would be too costly, requiring large numbers of troops to man it, the idea of cutting the Trail appealed to US Secretary of Defense, Robert S. McNamara. At that time, belief in the unlimited capabilities of technology was widespread and much US scientific research was already being devoted to advanced defense projects. It was assumed that the enemy's supposedly primitive military capability could easily be defeated by the might of US scientific ingenuity, which was, after all, about to put a man on the moon.

Four eminent scientists from Harvard and the Massachusetts Institute of Technology (MIT) were encouraged to explore scientific solutions. They proposed an $800m, airpower-supported barrier using electronic sensors monitored by aircraft to detect movement on the Trails and trigger immediate air attack. McNamara, who was worried that the stop-go *Rolling Thunder* effort was not achieving its intended purpose, became attracted to this hi-tech solution in October 1966 and Lt Gen Alfred Starbird was given command of the project. Senior USN and USAF commanders felt that mining Haiphong harbor and cutting the North's rail links with China would be more effective ways of restricting supplies for the Trail traffic, but these options were rejected by Johnson, who feared Chinese or Soviet retaliation. Although the anti-infiltration barrier idea was implemented, its limited success meant that the war on the Trails became one of relentless attrition against elusive targets, with some successes against the seemingly unstoppable flow of traffic.

ATTACKER'S CAPABILITIES
Spectres haunting Southeast Asia

The electronic fence

Early in 1966, Trail targets were identified by aircraft ranging from Air America "Butterfly" Pilatus PC-6 Turbo Porters operating from primitive Laotian forward airbases to direct strikes by A-1 Skyraiders, Royal Thai AF T-28Ds, and Thailand-based F-105 Thunderchiefs. The Porters, operated by Air America, Continental Air Services, and Bird and Son under CIA auspices were STOL (short takeoff and landing) stalwarts that flew an extraordinary range of missions throughout the war including FAC, reconnaissance, and even "bombing" trucks with rocks and hand grenades. Traffic had to be attacked piecemeal whenever it was detected and a more comprehensive solution was clearly needed. The anti-infiltration barrier proposed in June 1966 at the Institute of Defense Analyses JASON Summer Study session in Wellesley, Massachusetts at Robert McNamara's request, became increasingly appealing. *Rolling Thunder* had not brought Hanoi to the negotiating table or reduced the flow of supplies to VC forces. While General Westmoreland and Admiral Sharp advocated increased conventional firepower to erode the North's military capability, McNamara instead funded US Army development of an electronic barrier.

The four JASON study group scientists, Carl Kaysen, George Kistiakowsky, Jerome Wiesner, and Jerrold Zacharias, had considerable experience of electronic detecting devices; the precursors of a massive range of technical innovations from US laboratories for locating hostile forces. McNamara supervised the Advanced Research Projects Agency (ARPA) within the Defense Department and its inventions for the "gadget war" were developed in Project *Agile* and field-tested by the Army Concept Team in Vietnam (ACTIV), the USAF's Tactical Air Warfare Center at Eglin AFB, Florida, and a USN facility at Coronado, California.

Acoustic sensors, adapted from Project *Jezebel* anti-submarine sonobuoys and promoted by the Defense Communications Planning Group in Washington, were placed at precise locations along the Trail, ready to detect the sounds of passing traffic. Tactical aircraft distributed thousands of tiny micro-gravel mines whose detonations, when triggered by

Demonstrating its continued value, a Royal Thai Air Force T-28D (137802) awaits takeoff at Ubon RTAFB on September 1, 1972, while a 497th TFS F-4D with AN/ARN-2 LORAN-D and a massive AN/AVQ-11 Pave Sword laser-targeting pod on its centerline pylon passes through arming checks. (USAF)

T-28Ds accurately delivered napalm, rockets, 120lb fragmentation bombs, 100lb phosphorus bombs, and gunfire from 0.50-cal machine-gun pods. Larger ordnance made the aircraft unstable in an attack dive. Occasionally, they dropped their four Mk 24 flares, hoping to ignite a truck. (USAF)

wheels or footsteps, were picked up by the sensors and relayed to a patrolling aircraft overhead. JASON discussions acknowledged that the technology was not faultless and that the enemy would find ways of removing or bypassing the sensors. They also realized that antiaircraft weapons would be positioned to ambush the attack aircraft and sensor-droppers.

McNamara persuaded his Joint Chiefs of Staff to accept a Strong Point Obstacle System barrier in September 1967, despite its $800m per annum cost and doubts about its practicality. His statistical attitude to the war was supported by his calculations of likely aircraft losses relative to the cost of the operation compared with the heavy attrition suffered by US aircraft during *Rolling Thunder*. By December 1967, with his reputation damaged by the limited outcome of *Rolling Thunder*, McNamara instigated operational testing of the electronic barrier within a complex of minefields, barbed wire, and sentry points, constructed from April 1967. This physical barrier across Quang Tri Province, just south of the DMZ, included a network of acoustic sensors, short-range radar units, and infrared intrusion detectors, installed and supervised by troops. The first consignment of sensors for covert operational trials was shipped by the end of 1967 and up to 15,000 South Vietnamese villagers were relocated.

That project was disrupted by the lack of adequate roads, lorries, and building materials, and by constant attacks from long-range NVA artillery. It was then restricted to a physical "barrier" at four strongpoints: Khe Sanh, Con Thien, Gio Linh, and Camp Carroll. Interdiction of the intervening supply routes would be undertaken by USMC and US Army patrols rather than sensor-based air attack. Many sensors from the barrier were transferred to the USMC Khe Sanh outpost when it was besieged by the NVA in January 1968. Together with air-dropped examples, they formed a ring of 250 sensors near the base, which saved many Marine lives and led to further funding for operational use in Laos.

Air delivery

The barrier effort was instead refocused on the *Igloo White* program in Laos, where Operation *Steel Tiger* was gathering momentum in 1967. It became the technical basis for *Commando Hunt*, an integrated attack system to deal with Trail traffic involving air-delivered sensors, aerial reconnaissance and attack, and belts of landmines. Its success was inevitably limited by the vastness of the Trail area and by lack of knowledge of the roads and paths that were actually in use. A fully coordinated effort was not achieved until 1971, when the Infiltration Surveillance Center (ISC) at Nakhon Phanom RTAFB, near the Laotian border, had amassed enough relevant data.

Aircraft dropped two types of sensor on the southern Laotian Trails. Both were constructed with common integrated circuit modules for transmitting, decoding, and receiving messages. A seismic sensor called the Air Delivered Seismic Intrusion Detector (ADSID), or Spikebuoy in US Navy terminology, was a camouflaged 25lb dart-like projectile with a spring-steel antenna resembling tropical foliage protruding from its tail. The Acoustic Seismic Intrusion Detector (ACOUSID) (Acoubuoy I) version was dropped by a parachute which became caught up in tree branches, suspending the sensor above an area for surveillance. Its acoustic detector, like ADSID, gave around 30 days of continuous use from its lithium battery. ACOUSID also had a seismic detector and, like other sensors, it had to be dropped in such a way that a chain of sensors was installed at exact coordinates. An initial test was made by Misty F-100F Super Sabre pilots who lit their afterburners at exactly predetermined points on the Trail so that the sound could be picked up by the sensors.

Tiny "Dragonstooth" mines resembling small rocks were dropped in the same areas from Douglas A-1E Skyraiders to provide a sonic warning of human or vehicular movement and establish truck park locations by determining where the "movers" stopped. Mines were dispensed in a row between two columns of white smoke from a FAC's marker rocket (usually launched in a dive from 5,000ft at several miles range) in the same way as sensor deliveries from F-4Ds. Unfortunately, the mines were often degraded by rainfall and humidity. Trail travelers regarded them only as a nuisance. Both Phase I sensor types had a timer to catch activity at night when most would occur, or they could be kept active continuously.

The sensors' data was transmitted to a patrolling Lockheed EC-121R "Bat Cat" aircraft. Their information was then passed to the *Eagle White* or *Muscle Shoals* control personnel at the massive ISC for analysis by IBM 360/40 and model 1401 computers, which helped to determine the location of the sounds in relation to any sensors which had registered movement. The computers stored all sensor data, which was examined and evaluated on TV screens by Assessment Officers of the Communications Data Management Center, the "Dutch Mill," within the *Igloo White* program, who could monitor the entire "instrumented battlefield."

US Secretary of Defense Robert S. McNamara. Following his restricted bombing policy during *Rolling Thunder*, which hardened the North's resolve, McNamara sought more "humanitarian" solutions such as *Igloo White*. (US DoD)

The components of a "Spikebuoy." Its pointed steel forward quarter allowed the device to embed itself partially in the ground. (US Navy)

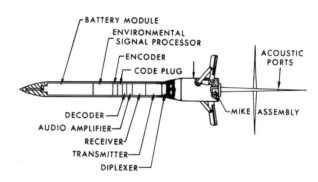

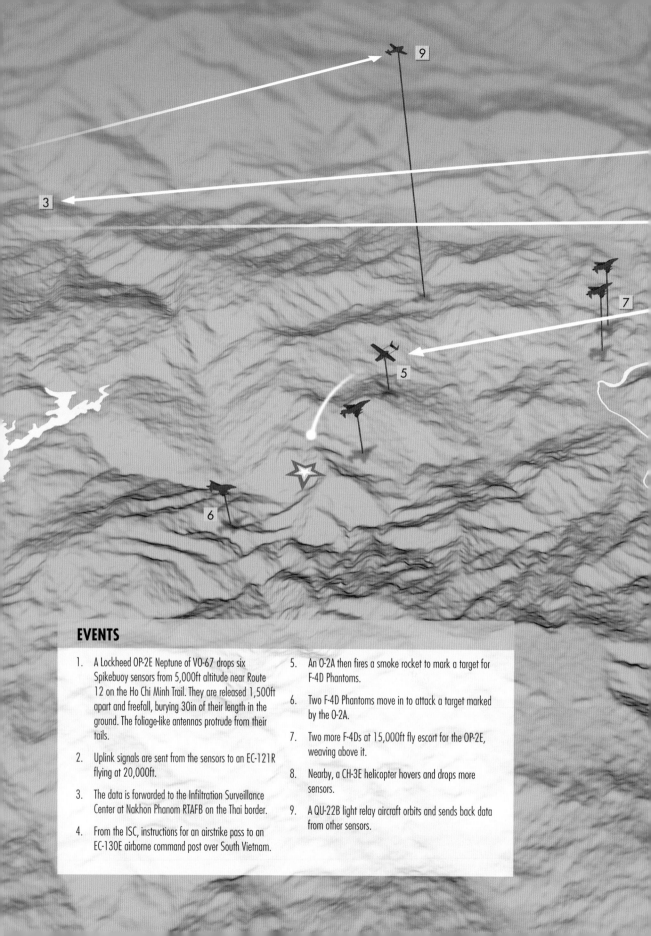

EVENTS

1. A Lockheed OP-2E Neptune of VO-67 drops six Spikebuoy sensors from 5,000ft altitude near Route 12 on the Ho Chi Minh Trail. They are released 1,500ft apart and freefall, burying 30in of their length in the ground. The foliage-like antennas protrude from their tails.

2. Uplink signals are sent from the sensors to an EC-121R flying at 20,000ft.

3. The data is forwarded to the Infiltration Surveillance Center at Nakhon Phanom RTAFB on the Thai border.

4. From the ISC, instructions for an airstrike pass to an EC-130E airborne command post over South Vietnam.

5. An O-2A then fires a smoke rocket to mark a target for F-4D Phantoms.

6. Two F-4D Phantoms move in to attack a target marked by the O-2A.

7. Two more F-4Ds at 15,000ft fly escort for the OP-2E, weaving above it.

8. Nearby, a CH-3E helicopter hovers and drops more sensors.

9. A QU-22B light relay aircraft orbits and sends back data from other sensors.

Igloo White

Igloo White, the electronic fence across the Ho Chi Minh Trail, initially required sensors to be dropped by OP-2E Neptunes. Their data was monitored by an EC-121R flying at 20,000ft and passed to Nakhon Phanom airbase in Thailand which issued instructions for an airstrike via an EC-130E ABCCC aircraft and an O-2A forward air controller.

2

4

1

8

Aircraft

OP-2E Neptune
EC-121R Warning Star
EC-130E Airborne Battlefield Command and Control Center
O-2A Skymaster
F-4D Phantoms
QU-22B Pave Eagle
CH-3 Sea King

O-1E 56-2667 "Lil' Puff" with marker rockets on 200lb-rated pylons. Pilots could drop smoke marker grenades from the cockpit window. The three on-board radios were a challenge to operate under stress and poor overhead vision could cause mid-air collisions. Rockets were aimed by aligning the horizon with a point between the second and third bolts on the central windshield support. (USAF)

Lt Col George Weiss described the process of analysis:

Each of the roads used by the North Vietnamese in [the Assessment Officers'] area is etched on his screen. As the seismic and acoustic sensors pick up the truck movements their locations appear as an illuminated line of light called 'the worm' that crawls across his screen, following a road that sometimes is several hundreds of miles away. From there the battle becomes academic. The Assessment Officer (AO) and the computer confer on probable times the convoy or convoys will reach a pre-selected point on the map. This point is a 'box' selected by the Igloo White team. Airborne at that moment are gunships and fighters. A decision is made as to the type of ordnance best suited for the area. If the trucks are moving under jungle canopy it is likely the AO will select fighters armed with CBU-type weapons and attack the convoy with them. If the convoy can be caught in an open area, then gunships will be waiting for them.

If a likely target was unlikely to move far, an EC-130E Airborne Battlefield Command and Control Center (ABCCC) was alerted. It called in strike aircraft, artillery, or even B-52s. Maj Gen William McBride, commanding Task Force Alpha at Nakhon Phanom ("Disneyland East" in pilots' parlance), controlled the *Igloo White* operation. During 1968, there was a systemic problem of command and control, with targeting being handled by Saigon as well as Task Force Alpha so that in March of that year only 15 percent of sensor detections were followed up by airstrikes.

The initial sensor tests required two stages: one for detecting trucks and a second to evaluate the sensors' success in recording troop movements. The first was performed during December 1967 in the Mud River valley area south of the Mu Gia Pass, around concentrations of road traffic at this choke point. A string of sensors was emplaced to assess movement over a stretch of road. It yielded successes both in detecting and attacking truck convoys, and to some extent in performing the role of a human observer. For Col McCoskrie, commanding the 56th Air Commando Wing at Nakhon Phanom RTAFB (known as "Ambassador Sullivan's Air Force"), a sensor was, "a soldier with infinite courage." For the pedestrian surveillance tests in an area between the DMZ and the Laotian border little was achieved, because most of the available sensors were transferred to Khe Sanh's defense.

Encouraging results in the Phase I tests led to a more capable Phase II series of devices with multiple command options. ACOUSID II allowed the Task Force Alpha operators at Nakhon Phanom to activate its microphones to listen out for truck movements at times when their experience suggested that movement was likely. They could be turned on in response to commands from Alpha controllers or made to record data showing a total of sensor detections over several days. This prolonged their battery life for up to 60 days. Fighter Aircraft Delivered Seismic Intrusion Detector (FADSID) was a successor to ADSID, designed to be dispensed by fighter aircraft such as the F-4D Phantom II, but it often proved incapable of surviving a high-speed air drop, so the previous ADSID remained in use.

A sensor falls away from an OP-2E Neptune. Its geophone transducer was sensitive enough to distinguish the vibrations of a truck at 300ft from those of human footsteps at 30ft range. (US Navy)

Phase III versions of the sensors appeared in 1969, offering a wider range of channels for the EC-121Rs to monitor and "Commike" microphones, which enabled the command center to listen in to conversations between troops or truck drivers. These devices were joined by other command microphone installations and engine ignition detectors. The latter, based on the airborne Black Crow sensor that could detect electrical emissions from unshielded petrol (not diesel) engines, cost around $3,000 each compared with $1,452 for an ACOUSID. In one test, 44 engine detectors were "sown" to check their accuracy against other sensors and they proved to be accurate in 80 percent of comparisons.

As the sensors could register movement within a radius of a mile, it became difficult for the interpreters to pinpoint the source of the signals unless they knew the exact position of the sensor within a chain of up to 15 devices. They also required close knowledge of the area through photo-reconnaissance images to relate that data to the actual topography.

Sensors could be dropped from A-1 Skyraiders or CH-3 helicopters. A helicopter drop of sensors from the hover was extremely accurate, but so was the ground fire that this method attracted. CH-3 drops continued in safer areas until February 1969. In November 1967, the main responsibility passed to the US Navy's VO-67 squadron, operating a dozen OP-2E Neptunes. They were converted from SP-2H standard to carry an AN/ALE-29 chaff dispenser and an AN/APQ-131 radar in place of their AN/APS-20E search radar dome beneath the forward fuselage. The long rear fuselage extension for the anti-submarine magnetic anomaly detector (MAD) was deleted. Camera and machine-gun stations were added together with long-range navigation (LORAN) equipment. Fighter escort was usually provided for their low-altitude sensor-drops.

A less successful sensor experiment involved the XM-2 "people sniffer," a device that was tested in a 196th Light Infantry Brigade UH-1 helicopter. It was supposed to detect particles of atmospheric pollution caused by smoke or any human emissions containing ammonia. Unfortunately, it could not distinguish between friend, foe, or animal. To prevent airstrikes on animal excretion in dense jungle and to protect the slow, low-flying sniffer UH-1 from

Two BLU-1 firebombs fall from SVAF A-1E 52-133882, which also carries ten 100lb white phosphorus bombs and two more BLU-1s. 1st Air Commando "fat face" A-1Es were initially used as FAC aircraft in 1966 but their enormous ordnance loads and long loiter time made them more useful as attackers, particularly against difficult targets such as storage caves. (USAF)

ground fire, the idea was abandoned in 1971. Smaller MINISID Miniaturized Seismic Intrusion Detector (MINISID) and Patrol Seismic Intrusion Device (PSID) acoustic sensors were also produced for use by ground troops.

Rain of bombs

Weather permitting, regular bombing of vulnerable sections of the network, particularly choke points and junctions, was the main US tactic. A meeting of three Trails at Dong Loc was typical in that respect. Vietnamese records claim that it was hit by 46,300 bombs in an eight-month period in 1968, with several attacks each day. For truck attacks, incendiary bombs, sometimes combined with napalm, seemed the most destructive weapons. The 926lb M36 incendiary "funny bomb" (known in World War II as the "Tokyo Firebomb") scattered 182 thermite bombs over a wider area than napalm. It was generally regarded as the best anti-truck weapon but supplies ran out after production ended in 1967 and a new version was not available for a year.

Col Frank Gailer, commanding the 35th TFW during *Commando Hunt*, estimated that, "when the M36 [incendiary] was available our truck kills were five times higher than the kills obtained after the supply was exhausted." The record of the M36 Destructor version was less impressive but it was still the most useful weapon for the purpose.

Spooky and the Shadows

Gunship helicopters and fixed-wing aircraft were in many ways the most effective US weapons in the Vietnam War. Over the Trails, gunships soon became as feared by the enemy

Veteran AC-47D 45-0927 with the "Spooky" nose-art worn by several 4th SOS gunships. The low-mounted wing limited the placement of gun positions. Gun-aiming required considerable skill. Pilots had to allow for wind and gun recoil, and calculate slant range. (USAF)

as the B-52s, although their power was exerted more forensically than the sledgehammer blows of Strategic Air Command's (SAC's) *Arc Light* attacks. Transport aircraft had already been converted for bombing roles, including Air America C-7 Caribou transports which dumped up to 14 field-constructed "Hot Soup" napalm canisters on Viet Cong positions, or C-130s using BLU-82B/C 15,000lb "Daisy Cutter" bombs to clear forest landing sites for helicopters. The venerable Douglas C-47 was the first type to be converted as airborne artillery, with armament fired sideways at ground targets as it orbited in a "pylon turn" maneuver. Project *Tailchaser* had used a C-131B with a GAU-2/A minigun mounted in the rear door and firing to the left for counter-insurgency operations. A missionary in South America invented the pylon turn as a way of delivering supplies to inaccessible villages. He lowered a rope attached to a bucket containing the goods and flew a circular orbit, keeping the bucket in the same position so that it was accessible to villagers.

This technique could be used to concentrate machine-gun fire on a small area and eventually to focus a laser target marker for delivery of guided weapons. Clearly, flying slowly in such a predictable way at around 4,000ft put the gunship at risk even at night, a factor which Tactical Air Command (TAC) saw as a reason to abandon the project during testing at Eglin AFB, Florida. However, C-47s were already using similar orbiting maneuvers in combat to deliver flares and incendiary target-marking "logs;" 18in. wooden blocks with magnesium cores.

Capt Ronald W. Terry persuaded Air Force Systems Command (AFSC) to revive the gunship idea in Project *Gunship I*. He supervised the field conversion of two aircraft with up to ten sideways-firing Browning M2 0.3 or four 0.5-cal machine guns, operated by the pilot. C-47D 44-8462 was converted to carry a single sideways-firing minigun pod but the GAU-2/A miniguns were in short supply at the time. On November 2, 1964, he established an AC-47 (originally dubbed "FC-47," a fighter designation, to the annoyance of many fighter pilots) test unit at Bien Hoa AB after Gen Curtis LeMay ordered operational testing of a converted C-47 mail-carrier, 48-48579 with three General Electric SUU-11A/A 7.62mm minigun pods and 24,000 rounds of ammunition. Initial daylight missions from December 15 used a FAC to select transport targets, but slow speed, excessive weight, and tail-heavy trim put AC-47Ds at a serious disadvantage over heavy defenses.

After consideration of the Convair C-131B (a testbed for a side-mounted minigun in 1963) and Convair 240/T-29 as possible "Gunship III" platforms, development of gunship versions of the Lockheed C-130 Hercules and Fairchild C-119 Flying Boxcar began in 1966. Lockheed AC-130A "Gunship II" conversions eventually became the primary gunships in Laos from 1968, but their sophisticated armament and detection systems took months to refine and they were initially used mainly for armed reconnaissance over the Trail. Technical problems included the accumulation of gun-smoke inside the fuselage, requiring improved

An AC-119K firing a minigun. A 20kW xenon searchlight is visible in the rear opening, with the AN/APQ-133 beacon tracking radar fairing ahead of the door. The ten-man crew flew 6.5-hour armed reconnaissance missions at 3,500ft, with two 1st SOS A-1 escorts following them, ready to attack any AAA site that fired at the gunship. (USAF)

venting. There were shortages of the heavily committed C-130s, so more plentiful Fairchild C-119s, already reallocated to USAF Reserve units, became gunships too. After the conversion of 26 examples into AC-119G Shadows in Project *Combat Hornet*, with four GAU-2/A miniguns, a night observation sight, and a 20kW AVQ-8 Xenon searchlight, they entered combat operations in January 1969 with the 71st Special Operations Squadron (SOS).

The uprated AC-119K Stinger added two podded General Electric J85 jet engines to the existing pair of 3,500hp Wright R-3350 radial engines. They compensated for the aircraft's increased weight and poor takeoff and single-engine performance owing to the addition of two M61 20mm cannon and an AN/APQ-136 search radar. Endurance was increased to 6.5 hours. Jury-rigged SUU-11/A pods for the GAU-2/A miniguns were replaced by Emerson MXU-470/A mountings, already installed in some AC-47s, and Stingers were also updated with AN/APN-147 Doppler navigation radar, AN/APQ-133 sideways-looking beacon tracking radar, and an AN/AAD-4 forward-looking infrared sensor, making them far more sophisticated hunters than the AC-47.

Unlike the AC-47, the AC-119K offered armor protection for the crew and AN/APR-25 and APR-26 ECM equipment together with an LAU-74/A flare-launcher with 24 rounds (reducing the AC-119G's 50,000 rounds of ammunition to a more-than-adequate 31,500 rounds) to illuminate targets at night. Fairchild-Hiller completed 26 C-119K conversions.

Gunship II

Large transport aircraft were not obvious candidates for conversion into heavily armed strikers, but the biggest gunship conversion, the AC-130 Hercules, was the most effective despite its lack of maneuverability. It was already one of America's most versatile pieces of equipment, including among its many roles "trash hauler," command and control vehicle, drone-launcher, weather reconnaissance, and tanker. On one sortie during the 1975 evacuation of Saigon, a C-130A with a single pilot carried 452 people to Thailand. As a gunship, its capacious cargo bay allowed the installation of more sophisticated target-detecting equipment and much heavier armament comprising four M61 Vulcan 20mm cannon and four XMU-470 7.62mm miniguns, all of which could fire out sideways from under the high-mounted wing

The same ZiL 157 trucks which had struggled along the Ho Chi Minh Trail for years were also among the first to bring troops to Saigon when the city fell to the North Vietnamese in April 1975. During the war, the strongly constructed Soviet trucks were often dragged off the Trail and repaired or cannibalized if they were hit by US ordnance. (Jean-Claude Labbe via Getty Images)

in a 30-degree left bank at around 5,000ft altitude. Longer endurance over target areas was also a major advantage. Conversion of early "Plain Jane" C-130As by E-Systems began with the decade-old JC-130A 54-1626 and included the first production Hercules 53-3129, which was not retired until September 1995. Detection equipment included a night observation device (NOD) that intensified light emissions by up to 60,000 times and a Xenon searchlight which could operate in either visible or infrared modes. ECM pods and chaff/flare dispensers could be hung on outboard wing pylons.

To cope with the increasingly effective NVA defenses, a modified Surprise Package version of the AC-130 prototype with USN M1 40mm Bofors antiaircraft guns in place of two of the 20mm guns, a far more capable digital computer, and an AN/AVQ-18 Pave Way I laser or TV designator for LGBs arrived at Ubon in December 1969. The longer-ranging 40mm guns used manually loaded four-round clips fired at 120rpm, which enabled the aircraft to shoot at a safer 14,000ft distance from AAA. The aircraft's truck kill rate increased to 7.34 per sortie and five aircraft were updated with Surprise Package.

Also in 1969, the AN/ASD-5 Black Crow passive direction-finding radar receiver to detect truck ignition-circuit radio frequency emissions was tested in a Blind Bat C-130 and subsequently installed in AC-130s, identifiable by a dome and a plate antenna on the left side of the nose. The device could detect trucks hidden under a jungle canopy. An ASQ-145 low-light TV camera was also fitted. The modified aircraft was rated by Tactical Air Command (TAC) as "the single most effective truck killer in SE Asia" and it returned to service at the end of 1970. Its improved sensors, particularly the IR unit, were particularly appreciated by its crews. However, it was acknowledged that the introduction of many 85mm radar-directed guns to Laos jeopardized the AC-130's role. By January 1971, 11 other AC-130As were given cut-price Pave Pronto updates, adding the 40mm guns but omitting the digital computer and inertial navigation system.

In the Pave Spectre program, 11 FY 1969 C-130Es were converted to gunships at the Warner Robins Air Material Area in 1972 and deliveries to Ubon began on October 25, 1971. With more powerful engines, the AC-130E could carry heavier protective armor and more ammunition together with the Surprise Package updates. Two aircraft also had a standard 105mm howitzer fitted in place of the fourth 40mm gun in the Pave Aegis/Pave

Spectre II program. It allowed the aircraft to attack with heavy 44lb shells from over 10,000ft, twice the range of 20mm-only armament. On its first sortie, a single hit destroyed three trucks and, during a later mission defending the town of An Loc, 13 T-54 tanks were hit. The 40mm gun had to score a hit on a vehicle's engine or cab to do real damage.

AC-130Es also had an observation blister built into the rear cargo door for an observer to spot Surface to Air Missiles (SAMs) or AAA threats. Previously, the door was left open in flight and the Illuminator Operator had to hang over the edge to keep watch. Violent maneuvers would sometimes leave him dangling behind the aircraft on his safety tether. Unfortunately, the first Pave Aegis AC-130E was badly damaged by 57mm AAA a month after entering service and the gun was moved to AC-130E 69-6571, which was itself shot down by 57mm AAA on March 30, 1972. Two more howitzer-toting Pave Aegis aircraft were sent to Thailand in May. AC-130As also had a gated laser night TV unit, which sent a pulsed laser beam through jungle cover to seek reflective targets such as trucks. The new sensors and guns increased the truck kill rate to the point where many crews were claiming 25 vehicles per mission. AC-130s seldom worked with FACs (for whom getting caught in the gunships' "prop-wash" proved to be dangerous on several occasions) or flare-droppers, preferring to manage their own targets.

Tactical strikers

Thailand-based F-105 Thunderchiefs were the mainstay of the Seventh AF bombing campaign during Operation *Rolling Thunder* and they also flew many of the early Trail interdiction missions when they became the top military priority from November 1968. In 1969, they were given numerous missions in northern and central Laos, attacking troop concentrations. Compared with slower piston-engine types, B-57s, and F-105s, the early F-4B and F-4C Phantom IIs had a poor record for bombing accuracy over the Trail, partly because the risk of ground fire forced them to deliver bombs from higher altitudes than the pilots would have preferred. Their triple ejector bomb-racks also tended to scatter the bombs slightly in situations where extreme accuracy was required. The F-4D version had a radar bombing system to replace the visual attack capability of the earlier variants. Its back-seat weapons system operator could select up to 15 offset aiming points on his AN/APA-65 radar bombing system for a computer-controlled attack on a target from above cloud or in darkness. For better accuracy, some F-4C/D pilots preferred the SUU-16/A 20mm gun pod for truck attacks at low altitude.

In all night attacks, the difficulty of delivering bombs on unseen targets under flares at 400–450kt remained a near impossibility for many fighter pilots. Glare and strange reflections from the flares, disorientating mist, and vertiginous 30-degree dives into blackness made accurate bombing extremely difficult. Lack of training in night attack was also a problem. Maj Les Leavoy, commanding the 416th TFS (F-100D/F), commented that, "New pilots arrive with absolutely no night weapons delivery training. This is the most difficult training to try and expose pilots to in a combat theater. Trying to divert a flare-ship for this training sometimes involves weeks. This results in fighter units having … a pilot that is 50 percent qualified."

For daylight bombing, the FACs usually thought the visual attacks by A-4 Skyhawks, which had a particularly good reputation for bombing accuracy, A-1 Skyraiders, or (later in the war) A-7 Corsair IIs yielded more consistent results than those by F-4s. However, during *Commando Hunt III*, F-4 crews claimed 1,576 trucks destroyed, many of them during missions with C-130 Blind Bats. Their speed was no guarantee of safety. November 11, 1969 was one of the bad nights, with three F-4s being shot down over the Trail and four crewmen killed. Another three were lost on November 16.

Armed reconnaissance became a frequent commitment from 1965 with tactical air navigation (TACAN) to back up the F-4Cs' inertial navigation system. In a pair of F-4s, one carried Mk 24 flares in eight SUU-25/A dispensers while the second had bombs, often delivered in the dive-toss mode. The arrival of F-4Es at Korat RTAFB from November 1968 brought a gun-armed Phantom version and a reinforcement of dive-toss bombing as an accurate technique for the F-4 squadrons. 25th TFS ARN-92 LORAN-D-equipped F-4Ds worked as pathfinders for two other F-4s in *Commando Bolt* (or "Flasher") in May 1969, using data from *Igloo White* (also dispensed by the 25th TFS) for formation attacks in bad weather or darkness. The F-4 trio dropped CBU-24 or napalm in close formation at 480kt from a level flightpath, exposing them to gunners.

The Pave Way

F-4Ds were most accurate when working in pairs; one with a Pave Knife laser target marking pod and a second carrying laser-guided 2,000lb Mk 84 bombs. In the 1971–72 dry season, 8th TFW F-4Ds dropped 1,317 LGBs on trucks, AAA batteries, and choke points. Pave Knife, although somewhat cumbersome, proved to be an effective, reliable device which was impeded only by smoke or fog, or affected by water ingress into its electronics. Blind Bat C-130s (or AC-130s) later became very effective laser markers for 2,000lb LGBs dropped from F-4 Phantom IIs (using LORAN coordinates to find the target location) to destroy many trucks on the Trail areas where heavy AAA did not threaten the Blind Bats. Cloud would obscure laser marking so a Blind Bat had to fly below it while the F-4D remained above it at around 12,000ft. Eventually, the increasing AAA forced faster F-4s to be used as laser carriers.

Some missions were flown with a pair of F-4Es, one to laser mark a target located by the Tiger FAC F-4E and the second to drop a Pave Way I LGB. A mission on June 11, 1970, by a 469th TFS F-4E, marked a ZSU-23 AAA gun which had fired at several bombers attacking road targets. The gun was silenced with a single bomb. In a December 1971 mission, a 130mm gun in northern Laos was totally destroyed by a Mk 84 LGB direct hit even though the bomb did not explode.

Various flaring patterns were tried in the attempt to allow one-pass strikes. For one, an F-4 dropped up to 20 parallel to the Trail but over a mile away to draw flak. Alternatively, flares could be dropped in a zigzag pattern each side of the Trail to spread the illumination. In both cases, strike F-4s followed up to hit any targets that were revealed. However, pilots preferred to work with FACs if they were available.

A GBU-10 laser-guided 2,000lb LGB falls from a 497th TFS "Night Owls" LORAN F-4D-33-MC (66-8810). Pave Way LGB missions, guiding bombs from another F-4D equipped with an AVQ-9 Pave Light device, a Pave Spike pod, or the Pave Knife system, were usually flown by 25th TFS crews. (USAF)

OPPOSITE THE PROCEDURE FOR LASER-GUIDED BOMB ATTACKS ON TRAIL TRAFFIC AND A 37MM AAA SITE

1. In 1971, a 433rd TFS LORAN-equipped F-4D Phantom II with a AN/AVQ-10 Pave Knife pod marks an AAA gun target for a second F-4D carrying two Mk 84 LGBs. The bomb is dropped into a "basket;" a conical area of airspace within which it could be guided precisely to its target following the laser energy of the Pave Knife.

2. A 23rd TASS Pave Nail LORAN-equipped OV-10A from Nakhon Phanom RTAFB with a Pave Spot laser designator pod and night periscope marks Trail truck targets for Mk 84 LGBs from two 23rd TFS, 8th TFW Pave Phantom F-4Ds. Pave Spot acquired the target and passed data on LORAN coordinates, slant range, and elevation to the F-4D's LORAN-directed bombing computer. A Raven FAC OV-10A fires a smoke rocket to mark the target as additional visual guidance. The F-4s, dropping bombs in a 30-degree dive at 11,000ft and 300kt, aim for the first and last trucks in the convoy.

F-100Ds were the USAF's workhorse tactical attackers in South Vietnam until 1970, but some of their missions took them across to the Cambodian border and Laos. They made the first night attack sorties in Laos on January 22, 1965, with a Blind Bat flare-ship. A notable night mission by two 481st TFS "Huns" from Da Nang AB helped to drive a Viet Cong assault team away from a special forces surveillance camp at Bu Dop in July 1965. Attacking at low level with Blind Bat flares for illumination, Capt Norm Turner and Lt Paul Watson took out a row of eight heavy machine-gun positions that were firing into the camp. The heavy fuel consumption of all fast jets, particularly F-4s, gave them a short time on the target compared with aircraft using reciprocating engines, so FACs had to mark targets and supply BDA for them very quickly.

Fast FAC

The use of less vulnerable fast jets as FAC vehicles was pioneered by the US Marine Corps in 1966 using "Condole"-coded TF-9J Cougars (replaced by "Playboy" TA-4F Skyhawks) over the Ho Chi Minh Trail, armed with 20mm guns and Zuni rockets. USAF and USMC Fast FACs relied on keeping their airspeed above 400kt to defeat the AAA, which had made O-1s and O-2s so vulnerable over the Trail. "Playboy" tactics included a delay of ten minutes between passes over a potential target, so that NVA gunners would be off guard. They worked particularly effectively with all-weather A-6 Intruders. Their four-ship "Hammer" deep air support (DAS) missions used a TA-4F Fast FAC to locate enemy AAA, two F-4B Phantoms to bomb them, and an RF-4B Phantom to photograph the results. Only two "Playboy" FACs were lost in action over the Trail by September 15, 1970, when their operations in *Steel Tiger* ended.

F-100F Super Sabre Commando Sabre ("Misty FAC") two-seat, single-engine fast jets operated extensively over North and South Vietnam from 1967 and, from 1968, over northern Laos. Their missions gradually moved into southern Laos as the Trail situation deteriorated and their skill in target-spotting became legendary. Misty F-100Fs usually carried two "Willie Pete" rocket pods and 400 rounds of ammunition for their four 20mm guns, which were particularly effective in strafing trucks or AAA guns as targets of opportunity, although their main function was to bring in F-4s or F-105 bombers. With in-flight refueling, they could establish FAC or Rescue Combat Air Patrol (RESCAP) orbits for over eight hours if necessary at speeds up to 460mph, directing strikes by F-100Ds or other aircraft. During their missions the "electronic fence" yielded little useful data and they relied on their own knowledge and vision to find trucks.

The element of surprise that a single, fast-moving F-100F flying at low altitude could enjoy, catching troops or truck drivers off guard, resulted in many truck kills. Misty pilots used a series of Delta points (geographical landmarks on the Trail) to divide it into sections for reference purposes when calling in strikes via the EC-130 "Hillsboro" (or "Moonbeam" for night missions) airborne control aircraft. Many of these destroyed troublesome AAA sites.

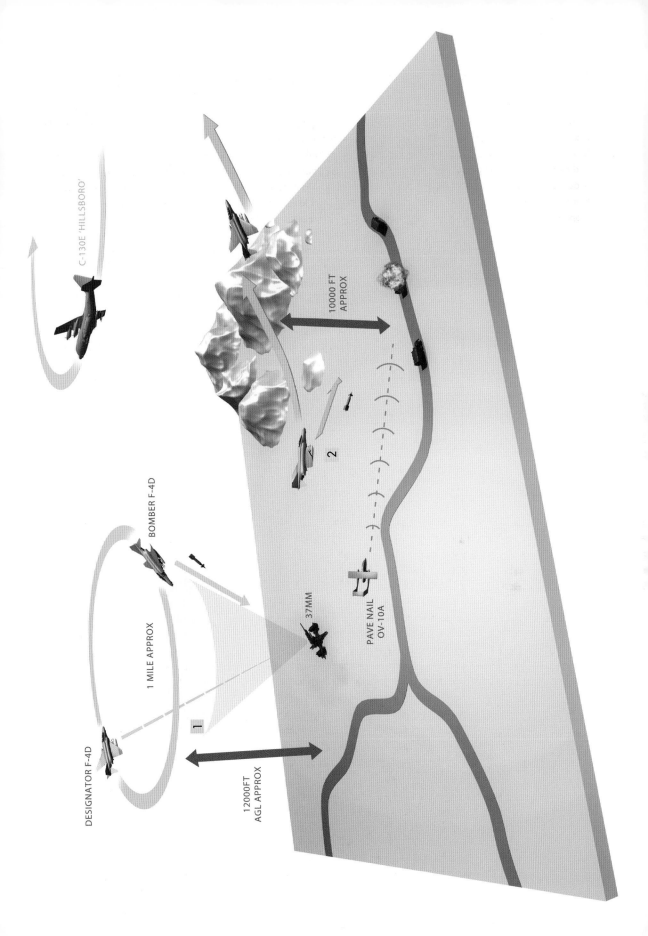

C-130E 'HILLSBORO'

DESIGNATOR F-4D

1 MILE APPROX

BOMBER F-4D

12000FT AGL APPROX

37MM

PAVE NAIL OV-10A

10000 FT APPROX

1

2

An A-1G (52-132665) of the 1st ACS, in VNAF markings, drops a white phosphorus bomb into dense forest on a trail route. This Skyraider was lost near Chavane, southern Laos, during an armed reconnaissance mission on February 14, 1966, killing Maj John Hills. (USAF)

From early 1969, Misty FACs experimented with Starlight scopes to find truck traffic from around 10,000ft altitude at night. The long, heavy scope was hard to operate in the back cockpit and it gave a narrow field of vision. If a convoy was found, the pilot dropped parachute flares for strike aircraft to begin their attack passes.

The more powerful F-4D/Es "Stormy FAC," "Wolf FAC," and "Tiger FAC," FAC with inertial navigation system and higher speed, gradually replaced the dwindling F-100Fs, using their speed to reduce the risk of ground fire in the more heavily defended Trail sections. They lacked the maneuverability of the piston-engine FAC aircraft, the crews' downward vision was worse, and the engines' long smoke trails gave gunners an additional aiming point. F-4D/Es also escorted other Trails missions, although their heavy fuel consumption required frequent in-flight refueling. "Bullwhip" RF-4C reconnaissance Phantom IIs sometimes worked with 366th TFW or 432nd TRW F-4D Stormy FACs to provide photographs of likely targets. Unlike the more vulnerable Nail O-2A FACs, the F-4s were allowed to operate in areas where there was a strong possibility of SA-2 launches. "Wolf" FACs came from the 8th TFW at Ubon and like other Fast FAC operators, they used volunteer pilots with at least 100 combat missions. They developed a highly detailed knowledge of the terrain, noticing the minutest sign of enemy activity despite the high speed of their "trail-sniffing" F-4 overflights.

Tiger FAC F-4Es of the 388th TFW from Korat RTAFB began to control some *Barrel Roll* strikes by USAF or USN aircraft from March 1969. By that time, the AAA opposition in that sector was formidable and five F-4Es were badly damaged between September and December 1969. They provided target weather information for other less sophisticated FAC aircraft, working in marginal weather conditions themselves. By April 1969, they were flying two missions a day, leading strike flights of F-105s or F-4s, which introduced radar-fused CBU for their truck attacks. The

One of the most commonly used weapons was the Mk 4 2.75in "Willie Pete" white phosphorus or smoke marker rocket, with a green warhead. Seven are packed into a disposable reinforced cardboard launcher aboard a 612th TFS "Misty" F-100F 56-3865. This aircraft and its crew were lost on August 16, 1968, and another "Misty" with captains Charles Shaheen and Dick Rutan aboard was downed the following day, but both survived. (USAF)

F-4E Fast FAC rolled in on the target first to mark it with a rocket and a flight of F-105s or F-4s would follow five seconds later.

The 388 TFW also flew Panther night missions with two F-4Es, one carrying flares and CBU, and the other loaded entirely with ordnance and its internal 20mm gun. Escort flights for AC-130 gunships were also on their 1969 list, armed with 12 Mk 82 bombs to respond to the threat of ground fire. Using the gunners' tracer fire to locate the AAA battery, Tiger FACs attacked them using their computerized dive-toss bombing mode. Although they were ordered to maintain a minimum of 4,500ft, their mission was usually impossible unless they operated at much lower altitudes, although mission reports then had to be "modified" accordingly. They had to sustain speeds of 600mph, requiring frequent use of afterburner and consequently up to five in-flight refueling sessions per mission. At high speed, they were still expected to recognize the details of a potential target and determine whether it was hostile or friendly, a dilemma most often solved by whether or not it fired at the FAC.

Bronco

The North American OV-10A Bronco, the result of a long quest for an armed counter-insurgency aircraft, joined the FAC force in 1968 for Covey FAC missions to supplement O-2As and from June 1970 as "Rustic" FACs over Cambodia. 19th Tactical Air Support Squadron (TASS) "Rustics," flying from Bien Hoa AB (later, Ubon RTAFB with the 23rd TASS) usually carried a Cambodian observer and communicated in French. A number of Broncos were transferred from Da Nang to the 23rd TASS at Nakhon Phanom, operating with "Snort" call-signs. Its four M-60 7.62mm guns provided immediate close air support when required. In 1970, Seventh AF ordered the guns to be removed, stating that FAC pilots were using them at low altitude and putting themselves at risk from ground fire. The decision was reversed in September 1970. OV-10As became a highly maneuverable light attack aircraft for the USMC's river patrol missions and they provided vital support for covert Trail activities.

In the *Steel Tiger* area in 1970, Covey OV-10As took on most of the daytime missions, leaving the squadron's O-2As to cope with night FAC duties, although many OV-10A night missions were also flown using a Starlight scope. The scope's use was impeded by internal canopy reflections in the cockpit, so a curtain separated the cockpits to mask light from the instrument panel. By day, an OV-10A pilot flew with his binoculars, 35mm telephoto

OPPOSITE PRINCIPAL US AIRBASES IN SOUTHEAST ASIA AND MAIN AREAS OF AIR OPERATIONS OVER LAOS

Key:	
1.	Da Nang. USAF: **476th TFS** (F-104C, 1965), **777th TCS** (C-123, 1962) **3rd TFW** (F-100, 1965) **35th TFW** (F-100, 1965), **366th TFW** (F-4C/D, 1965–72), **20th TASS** (O-1, OV-10A (1965–72), **9th ACS** (O-2B, U-10D, AC-47D, 1967–72), **37th ARRS** (HU-16, HH-3, HH-53, HC-130H, HH-43B/F, 1966–72). USMC: **HMM-163/-162/-261/-361/-364/-365** (UH-34, 1962–65), **VMFA-531/-542/-513/-115/-212** (F-4 1965–72), **VMA (AW)-235/-242** (A-6A (1966–70), **VMCJ-1** (RF-8A, RF-4B, EF-10B, EA-6A (1965–75).
2.	Phu Cat. **37th TFW** F-100 and Misty FAC F-100F (1967–70, became 12th TFW, F-4D 1970), **4th ACS**, (AC-47 1967–69), **389th TFS, 480th TFS** (F-4C/D 1969–71), **18th SOS** (AC-119K 1969–70), **17th SOS** (AC-119G (1970–71), **361st TEWS** (EC-47N/P 1969–71), **38th ARRS Det 13** (1967–71), **459th TCS** and **537th TCS** (C-7A 1966–70).
3.	Tuy Hoa. **31st TFW** (F-100 1967–70), **136th TFS** and **188th TFS** ANG (F-100 1968–69), **71st SOS Flight A** (AC-119G 1969–70).
4.	Cam Ranh Bay. **43rd TFS** (F-4C 1965), **12th TFW** (F-4C 1965–70), **315th AD, 483rd TCW** (C-130A/E, C-7A 1965–72), **39th ARRS** (HC-130P 1970–71), **360th, 361st** and **362nd TEWS** EC-47N/P/Q, 1971–72).
5.	Phan Rang. **35th TFW** (F-100 and B-57 inc. RAAF Canberra B.20 1966–71), **366th TFW** F-4C/D (1966), **120th TFS** ANG (F-100 1968–69), **315th ACW** (C-123B/K 1967–71), **9th SOS** (O-2 1971–72).
6.	Bien Hoa. **3rd TFW** (F-100 1965–70), **350th SRS** (DC-130A, AQM-34, 1966–70), **1st ACS** (B-26, T-28, SC-47, A-1E, 1963–66), **19th TASS** (O-1 1963–72), **405th FW Dets** (B-57 1964–65), **38th ARRS Det 6** (HH-43B/F 1965–71), **604th ACS** (A-37A 1967), **4th SOS Det** (AC-47 1966–69), **12th SOS** (C-130 Ranch Hand 1965–69), **4080th SRW** (U-2A/C/F 1964–70).
7.	Tan Son Nhut. HQ 2nd AD, **460th TRW** (RF-101C, RF-4C, RB-57E 1966–71), **4th ACS** (AC-47 1965–66).
8.	U-Tapao. **4248th SW/ 307th SW** (B-52D/KC-135A 1966–75).
9.	Don Muang. **45th TRS Det** (RF-101C 1961–62), **6091st RS** (C-130B 1964), **509th FIS** (F-102A 1962–70), **4103rd ARS** (KC-135A 1972).
10.	Korat. **6234th TFW** (F-105D, F-100F 1965–66), **388th TFW** (F-105, F-4, EB-66C/E, EC-130E 1966–74), **354th TFW** (A-7D 1972–73), **553rd RW** (EC-121D/R 1967–70), **347th TFW** (F-111A 1974-1975), **16th SOS** (AC-130H 1974–75).
11.	Takhli. **27th TFW** (F-100 1961–65), **405th TFW** (F-100 1965), **6441st TFW** Provisional (F-105 1965), **355th TFW** (F-105, EB-66 1965–70), **474th TFW** (F-111A 1968), **49th TFW** (F-4 1972), **16th SOS Det.1** (AC-130 1972), **366th TFW** (F-4 1972), **474th TFW** (F-111A 1972–73).
12.	Ubon. **15th TFS** (F-4C 1965), **8th TFW** (F-4C/D, AC-130, AC-123 Black Spot, B-57G 1965–74), **315th ACW** (C-130A Blind Bat 1966-1970), **4th, 31st, 33rd TFW TDY Dets.** (F-4E 1972).
13.	Nakhon Phanom. **33rd ARS** (HH-43B 1964), **38 ARRS Det 1** (CH-3C 1965–66), **56th SOW** (A-1E/H/J, A-26A/K, C-123, U-10D, T-28D, O-1, O-2, OV-01A, AC-119, EC-47N/P/Q, EC-121R, QU-22, 1967–74), **23rd TASS** (Nail O-1, O-2, OV-10A 1966–75), **VO-67** (US Navy, OP-2E 1967–68).
14.	Udorn. **45th TRS** (RF-101C 1965–66), **555th TFS** (F-4C 1966), **432nd TRW** (AC-47D, SC-47D, U-10A, F-4D/E, RF-4C, EC-130E ABCCC, AC-119K, EB-66B/C, 1966–75).
15.	Nha Trang. **23rd SAWD** (OV-1 1962), **5th ACS** (C-47B/D, SC-47D, U-10 1966–69), **602nd ACS** (A-1E/H/J 1966), **5th Special Forces Group** (C-123B, C-47, CV-2 Caribou 1964), **14th SOW** , A-1E/G/H/J, B-26B, RB-26L, AC-47D, SC-47, T-28D, C-130E, AC-119G/K, O-1, O-2, OV-10A, A-37A/B, 1966–69).
16.	Pleiku. **604th ACS** (A-37A 1967), **4th ACS Det.** (AC-47D, SC-47 1966–69), **21st TASS** (O-1E/F/G, O-2A, U-10 1965–66), **1st ACS** (A-1E/H/J, B/RB-26B, SC-47, T-28D, SC-47 1966–67), **362nd TEWS** (EC-47N/P/Q 1967–72).
17.	Binh Thuy **22 TASS** (O-1E/F/G, O-2A 1965–71), **USN VAL-4** (OV-10A 1969–72), **38th ARRS Det.10** (HH-3E, HH-43B/F, HU-16B 1965–70).
18.	Marble Mountain Air Facility USMC **MAG-16** (UH-1, CH-46, CH-53 1965–71).
19.	Task Force 77. USN aircraft carriers offshore on Yankee Station.
20.	Task Force 77. USN aircraft carriers offshore on Dixie Station.
21.	Andersen AFB, Guam. Strategic Air Command B-52D/G and KC-135A/RC-135 units.

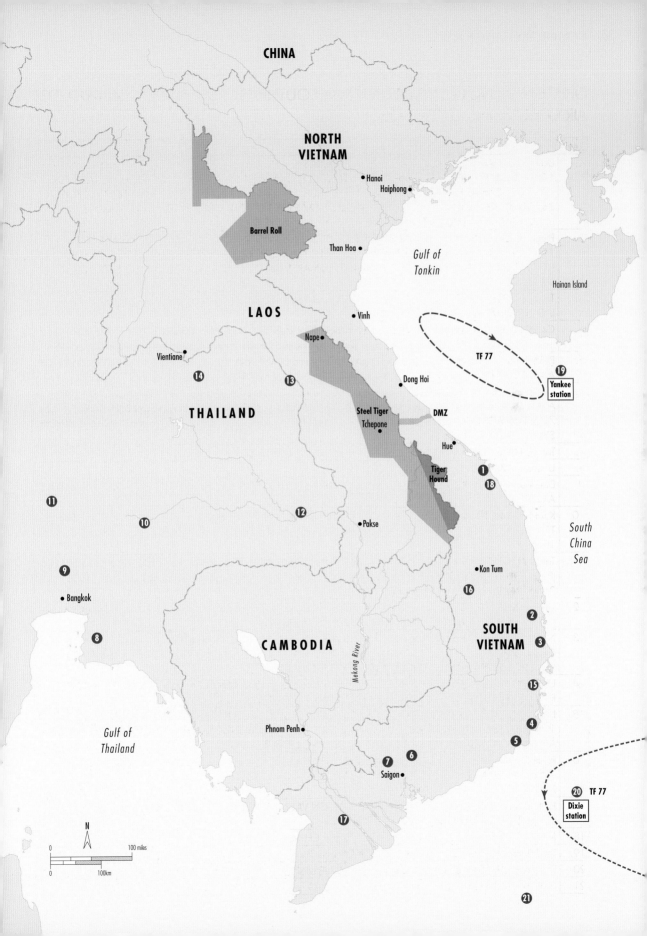

CHINA

NORTH
VIETNAM

• Hanoi
Haiphong •

Barrel Roll

Than Hoa •

Gulf of
Tonkin

Hainan Island

LAOS

• Vinh

Nape •

Vientiane •

14

13

THAILAND

Steel Tiger
Tchepone •

Dong Hoi •

TF 77

19
Yankee
station

DMZ

Hue •

Tiger
Hound

1

18

South
China
Sea

11

10

12

• Pakse

• Kon Tum

9

16

• Bangkok

2

8

CAMBODIA

SOUTH
VIETNAM

3

Mekong River

15

4

Gulf of
Thailand

5

Phnom Penh •

6

7

Saigon •

20 TF 77
Dixie
station

17

N

0   100 miles

0   100km

21

camera, and tape-recorder to hand, a clipboard of mission details on his knee, and five radios to manage. Lacking air conditioning, the cockpit temperature became oppressive during the day. For Cambodian "Rustic" missions, he also had to talk to his back-seater, who would be communicating with ground commanders in French.

In summer 1971, 15 23rd TASS OV-10As were fitted with low-light television equipment, Pave Nail laser target marking, and a radar transponder. Operating as target markers for F-4Ds, they initially achieved great success, destroying most of the enemy-held bridges in Cambodia and some crucial fords, road junctions, and traffic in Laos. Their performance was limited when the weather obscured the laser with fog and haze, but in mid-1972 they were coping with over half of the laser-guided bombing in SE Asia and participating in numerous search and rescue operations such as the famous effort to recover the navigator of EB-66 "Bat 21." Meanwhile, Raven FACs continued to fly the diminishing numbers of O-1 Bird Dogs in support of Laotian regular forces until 1972.

MACV-SOG

The OV-10A was 80mph faster than the less maneuverable O-2A's 190mph and it carried 3,600lb of ordnance. Despite the canopy's excellent daytime visibility, the back-seater's view was restricted and the curved canopy surfaces caused internal reflections at night, so the O-2A was preferred for night missions. (USAF)

While the USA would not commit large troop numbers to neutral Laos, focusing its efforts on the ground war in South Vietnam, it conducted a clandestine program of special forces operations there throughout the war. In 1964, South Vietnamese troops were used for this purpose in Operation *Leaping Lena*, but its lack of success left no option other than a small-scale, secret commitment of US soldiers. Teams from the OP35 team in the Military Assistance Command, Vietnam – Studies and Observations Group (MACV-SOG), using Green Beret troops, conducted Trail watch duties, bomb damage assessment, and Bright Light attempts to recover aircrew who had been shot down, or their remains. Despite the academic-sounding title and their highly detailed reporting techniques, SOG also led guerrilla missions to locate and cut the fuel pipelines that supplied trucks in Laos and destroy supply caches.

Their efforts in Laos as top secret "Spike Team" joint-service reconnaissance patrols from 1964 were increased and code-named "Shining Brass" (later, "Prairie Fire"), with "Daniel Boone" for covert Cambodian missions and "Nickel Steel" for risky ventures into the DMZ. CH-34 Kingbee or UH-1 Huey helicopters, often with South Vietnamese AF pilots, inserted and extracted the teams. O-2A or OV-10A FACs managed the operations, flying at treetop altitudes. Their activities behind enemy lines involved assassination of key enemy personnel, locating AAA sites, interception of trucks, planting sensors, and performing sabotage. Some even adopted Viet Cong or Pathet Lao uniforms and carried AK-47 rifles. They worked close to the Trail and accurately recorded the coordinates of camouflaged rest stations or supply dumps that they saw so that airstrikes could be called in.

Road-watch teams were also able to send weather reports via CIA radio channels, avoiding wasted missions owing to inadequate visibility over the Trail. From 1970, Covey OV-10A pilots flew "X-Ray" missions in which they collected a CIA-trained "Covey rider" special forces or Lao observer (picked up by CIA "Air America" aircraft) who would lead them to potential targets. By the end of 1970, SOG teams had become a priority target for NVA forces and 40,000 troops were positioned along the Trail to intercept them and neutralize their helicopter landing zones. SOG's strike element, Hatchet Force, used many Montagnard troops with US leaders. Occasionally, it required USMC CH-53 Sea Stallion helicopters with gunship and Covey FAC support for its long-range missions including Operation *Tailwind*, a raid on massive NVA supply dumps at Chavane. In 1970, SOG operated a Heavy Hook detachment (call-sign "Knife") at Nakhon Phanom with HH-53 helicopters for long-distance team extractions. SOG casualties were high for a small organization, with 29 Americans killed or missing in 1969 alone, and the missions became prohibitively hazardous as NVA forces multiplied. By October 1970, a quarter of the assigned Prairie Fire FAC pilots had been lost, but SOG operations continued into 1971 against ever-increasing opposition. Based at Ubon RTAFB, a number of OV-10A FACs with Nail and Rustic call-signs continued to fly missions over Cambodia and the Ho Chi Minh Trail until the official end of hostilities in February 1973.

A pair of "Big Jolly" HH-53Cs await their next call. The helicopter arrived in SE Asia in 1968 to replace the HH-3 "Little Jolly," providing longer range and bigger capacity. It could reach 11,000ft altitude, avoiding the lighter ground fire. (USAF)

DEFENDER'S CAPABILITIES
The deadly lifeline

North Vietnamese gunners fire their 57mm weapon as a USAF RF-101C Voodoo photographs the AAA site on February 25, 1966. Flying at low altitude at near-sonic speeds was the reconnaissance pilot's only defense against such heavy anti-aircraft opposition. (Underwood Archive via Getty Images)

The Ho Chi Minh Trail network could be seen as North Vietnam's biggest military asset and most important achievement in its effort to occupy South Vietnam. Despite its skill in using propaganda, Hanoi underplayed its ability to insert large numbers of troops into South Vietnam, preferring to promote the idea that resistance to the Saigon government came from within South Vietnam itself. For Gen Vo Nguyen Giap, victor at Dien Bien Phu and architect of the Trails, the network was an invaluable contribution to the war. However, it was also a voracious consumer of manpower with up to 120,000 men and women working to maintain the network, and building up to 60 miles of road per month in 1965–66. Up to 30,000 were killed and an equal number were seriously injured by air attack or through accidents, malaria, or dysentery. Of these, malaria (known as the "jungle tax") was the biggest killer and it was generally regarded as a much greater threat than American attacks. Many workers were persuaded into service from coastal farms or city life and had to adapt to the jungle, living in underground bunkers for up to ten years to avoid bombing. After the war, a cemetery for the known victims of the Trail covered some 40 acres and contained memorials for over 10,300 Vietnamese, but many thousands more died unrecognized. For Giap and his country, focused entirely on securing unification and independence, it was a worthwhile price. He stated that he was prepared to pay ten lives for every American killed. Hanoi's eventual estimate of losses amounted to around two million people.

The first fighters to make the arduous six-month journey in the stifling jungle humidity were Vietminh, heading for South Vietnam from Hanoi in great secrecy in May 1959. They were lucky to advance more than seven miles a day, wearing sandals made from motor tires, and many fell ill and had to be left in crude roadside shelters where most died. Some fell asleep with exhaustion as they walked, and many lost their hair and developed chronic arthritis from years in the jungle. Later in the war, the journey time was reduced to 40 to 50 days, and after preparations for the 1975 invasion were complete and the 24ft-wide, two-lane paved, 3,000-mile highway was opened, the journey could be made in 11 nights.

For the thousands who made up to two million journeys along the labyrinth of paths and roads, the main defenses against US attack were evasion and camouflage, with AAA guns to fend off attacks where possible. Gen Giap ordered that fences should be erected each side of the tracks so that climbing plants could grow up them, meeting to form a camouflage roof over the paths and disguising the infrared signature of vehicles. Rocks were attached to the branches to make them curve and meet over a track. USMC FAC pilots saw stretches of camouflaged Trail extending for up to 50 miles, identifiable only by slightly faded foliage.

By 1973, over 1,800 miles of roads had been camouflaged. Caves, used for shelter and storage, were disguised with foliage too and fake AAA sites and truck parks were constructed including dummy vehicles containing cans of fuel that ignited when hit by air attack and blinded the infrared sensors of gunships. Larger heavily defended caves, like the one in the so-called "Banana Karst" mountain near Ban Kengsep, were used for truck maintenance. Bridges could be constructed with stone slabs just beneath the water level of streams and small rivers, detectable only by an experienced FAC. Ferry barges were used for deeper water, but only at night.

AC-130 gunships were feared by truck drivers as their infrared sensors could detect the heat of an engine for some time after it had been turned off to try and evade detection. Cooking fires could also be detected by IR sensors or by smoke that could be noticed by a FAC pilot. To avoid that danger, the smoke was channeled away through bamboo pipes in trenches and filtered through leaves to dissipate it. In one attack, a traveler witnessed the deaths of 400 people in a convoy after cooking-fire smoke had alerted a FAC who called in a strike flight. In many ways, the most useful camouflage was provided by monsoon cloud cover. Even in dry season, cloud cover, fog, and smoke from undergrowth clearance for agriculture made aerial attack very difficult.

Bad visibility precluded most airstrikes and Misty pilots, who were accustomed to flying beneath the clouds, became used to seeing big increases in traffic when the Trail was protected by low cloud ceilings or heavy mist. Movement could be coordinated through the network of radio and telephone lines that were a vital part of the Trails plan. Attempting to monitor these messages became a major task for US intelligence agencies.

By day, the routes could seem deserted, but at night or during bombing pauses like the 1967 Christmas Truce, they were filled with traffic. Unexploded bombs or large craters could delay traffic and cause traffic jams that made attractive targets for bombers. Blockages therefore had to be cleared very fast, often a great risk to the volunteers who tackled the bombs. Misty FAC pilots were often amazed that badly damaged roads would be in use again the following day. The contents of damaged trucks or vehicles delayed by a road cut were rapidly reloaded onto replacement trucks. This all made accurate photo-reconnaissance information hard to acquire and assess, and the first-hand reports from experienced FACs often gave more reliable target information.

Because the original East Truong Son routes in Vietnam could become impassable owing to bad weather or enemy action, General Giap opened the Western route (West Truong Son or Ta Le) through the precipitous karst mountain terrain of Laos. Decoy trails were often left open and derelict vehicles were placed on them as tempting targets for US airmen, but there were also hidden AAA guns surrounding the trucks. Drivers soon learned to vacate their cabs if their vehicle was bracketed by a few sparkling "sighting" rounds of Misch ammunition from

General Vo Nguyen Giap, a former history teacher who became North Vietnam's "Red Napoleon" and major strategist from World War II until 1975. He commanded the Viet Minh and then the North Vietnamese Army, and became the prime mover behind the Ho Chi Minh Trail. His policy was to fight, literally, to the last man. (Getty Images)

Travelers on the Trail had the advantage of many underground command centers, hospitals, and rest centers, many of which escaped US detection during the war. Caves and tunnels contained auto repair workshops like this one, where damaged vehicles could be returned to the road. (Getty Images)

an AC-130, as this signaled the imminent arrival of a torrent of gunfire. It was also realized that Trails such as Route 15 through the mountains were safer than the French-built paved roads on the coastal plains. They were more likely to be protected by low cloud and rain, and their steep karst slopes made attacks by low-flying aircraft extremely hazardous. Monsoon cloud cover in any case required pilots to search for holes in the overcast through which they could dive to attack, but those holes also assisted AAA gunners as they awaited targets.

Firing back

As US air attacks intensified in 1965, General Dong Si Nguyen focused on the need to provide antiaircraft defenses along the Trails, supervised by Group 565. Compared with the sophisticated technology supplied to American pilots, the available AAA weapons were usually obsolescent Soviet and Chinese examples, most of which dated back to World War II or beyond. However, their effect on relatively unprotected airframes was potentially lethal. In many cases, a single 37mm hit could cripple a large aircraft, and this forced all aircraft to operate at higher altitudes than pilots preferred for achieving accuracy. Near the Plain of Jars in Laos, Raven pilots encountered Soviet-supplied BTR-40 armored vehicles with twin 14.4mm machine guns as well as 37mm M1939 weapons.

Around half the guns US pilots encountered in 1968–70 in southern Laos, marked as red circles on briefing maps, were mobile 37mm units whose seven-round streams of orange "beer can" shells seemed to move more slowly in darkness than the clusters of fiery red projectiles from 23mm guns. They were usually set to explode at 9,000–10,000ft and gunners moved the gun in azimuth as they fired to spread the shell-bursts. The rest were mainly twin-barrel 23mm, while the heavier 57mm guns, many of them radar-guided and a real threat to strikers, were emplaced at choke points such as the Mu Gia Pass where the Trail entered Laos.

At low altitudes, FAC pilots could expect to see the green tracers from AK-47 automatic rifles, sometimes from insurgents lying in wait near the ends of Lima-site runways to fire up at aircraft after takeoff. Pilots flying over Laos estimated that the number of guns placed along the supply routes more than doubled in 1968. The increase was rapid as mobile AAA guns were towed into position, many of them by battalions released from the defense of North Vietnam after the end of *Rolling Thunder*. An estimated 166 weapons were in the Trail region at the end of *Rolling Thunder* but that total rose to 621 four months later, together with gunners who had learned their trade well around Hanoi. Some were mounted on trucks within convoys, but all the lighter weapons could be towed to new locations and set up for action within ten minutes. Most belt-fed 23mm weapons could be broken down and hand-carried.

From 1970, some 52-K 85mm and KS-19 100mm guns were positioned around strategic areas such as road junctions. Whereas the smaller-caliber guns fired tracers which pilots could see at night, the big 85 and 100mm weapons fired single shells and only the initial muzzle flash (massive in the case of the 100mm weapon) might be noticed. Despite its other inherent dangers, the visibility of tracers made night-flying safer for pilots than operations by day, as the tracers revealed the gunners' positions. In the early years of the war, gunners knew that aircraft could attack them only if they fired at the attackers first.

In March 1968, the 388th TFW noted that 254 rounds had been fired at its Tiger FAC F-4Es. A month later, the total of ZU-23-2 23mm, M1939 37mm, and 57mm rounds had risen to 5,624 and it continued to increase throughout the year. One FAC estimated that there were up to 30 AAA guns per mile, mostly 37mm, on some sections of the Trail by 1969. These guns were hard to spot at night, as their tracers did not ignite until they were several hundred feet from the gun. Lighter weapons such as the 7.62mm Type 67 machine gun and 12.7mm DShK-1938 "Dushka" heavy machine gun (roughly the equivalent of a 0.50-cal gun and often regarded as the "helicopter slayer") were easily transportable and could be set up quickly to fire at low-flying attackers.

By 1971–72, one of the most feared weapons was the ZPU-4 14.5mm "Zip" gun, a reliable four-barreled towed weapon firing up to 2,400 rounds per minute and "hosing" bullets into

The tall triple-canopy forest provided excellent cover for vehicles during daytime. Trucks were camouflaged with branches and they tended to travel in groups of three or four at night. Caves were used for storage and rest areas, and their entrances were often disguised by foliage, making air attack very difficult. (Getty Images)

Lacerating fire from a ZPU-2 gun, at 400rpm, could "hose" a hundred 23mm rounds at an aircraft two miles away. The barrels (worn out after 10,000 rounds) then became too hot and had to be changed. The gun was easily transportable on its twin wheels. (Dr. Istvan Toperczer)

the path of aircraft flying below 3,000ft. By 1975, the NVA had received some ZSU-23-4 light tanks incorporating the four-barrel gun and its RPK-2 Gun Dish guidance radar.

Flak tactics

Although guns were transportable by road, their operators tried to set them up in well-camouflaged sites with good views from above the Trail. Hillsides gave gunners a better view of the attackers and presented more difficult targets for retaliatory bombing. They could bracket aircraft from both sides of a valley to counteract a pilot's attempts to "jink" and avoid their fire. On mountain passes, guns were arranged in a box formation, with two each side of a likely attack point. Heavy machine guns were often arranged in a triangular pattern beside Trail routes to concentrate their fire. Where possible, gun crews established a shelter in a cave from which a light gun such as a 14.5mm ZPU "Zip" gun could be quickly wheeled out and fired. In Cambodia, pagodas, off-limits as targets, were often used to store munitions and hide AAA weapons.

Gunners were consistently successful in frustrating many of the US attempts to monitor movement on the Trail, particularly those using slower aircraft that might otherwise have detected far more traffic activity. Many attempts to use EC-47 electronic reconnaissance aircraft to locate radio transmitters in Laos or to use airborne direction finding to establish targets for B-52s were curtailed when AAA jeopardized the old piston engine aircrafts' role. AC-130s and their escorts were primary targets for AAA and gunners barrage-fired at both during an attack.

AAA crews tried to hide their positions, especially at night when their muzzle flashes were more visible. They listened to the engine note of attack aircraft, assisted by home-made devices incorporating two megaphones, a bamboo tube, and earphones. They waited for the change in sound of reciprocating engines that indicated that the aircraft had entered an attack dive, before firing at them. Consequently, flak-suppression efforts often sought to deafen gunners with explosions, particularly of 2,000lb bombs, rather than destroy their weapons.

Imminent air attacks would be signaled by telephone, gunshots, or whistles, repeated from sentinel to sentinel along the route. US pilots were often impressed by the gunners' good fire

discipline, as they would fire only to defend specific targets. The difficulty in resupplying them with ammunition necessitated economy with the bullets, a discipline encouraged by Ho Chi Minh himself. Strike pilots often defied advice to avoid dueling with AAA guns unless they were seen as a persistent threat to other strikers.

Despite severe ill health in his final years, Ho Chi Minh visited his AAA gunners, including this 57mm crew, to inspire and encourage them. (Getty Images)

Steel crows

Teams of female sappers were positioned on the routes to defuse unexploded US munitions. Others, often young girls, were constantly filling in the craters caused by bombs from B-52s (known as "steel crows") and other attackers. Travelers learned how to identify bombs by the sound they made; CBU "mother bombs" landed with a thud after releasing their "baby bombs" while LGBs' tail units made a clattering sound as they steered the bomb to its target. Sappers' expertise rendered a proportion of US ordnance ineffective. Mk 36 aerial magnetic mines, which could demolish a truck, were often located and defused, and miniature gravel detonators were merely regarded as a nuisance. The wide range of anti-personnel mines

Hitting caves on the Trail

A Douglas A-26A "Counter-Invader," 64-677 flown by Maj Al "Batman" Shortt and Capt Larry Counts of the 609th Special Operations Squadron "Nimrods" makes an interdiction napalm strike under forward air control (FAC) on a camouflaged storage cave at the base of a mountain in 1969. Previous attempts had failed and the FAC pilot asked the Nimrod crew to hit the cave opening. Identifying the exact location by partial moonlight was difficult. In a low-angle attack, their first two BLU-1 napalm canisters fell short and they increased the speed and altitude of their next run. One canister exploded on the cave's edge. Fire flowed into the cave, triggering secondary explosions. Many caves in Laos were used to store supplies and weapons for Trail transportation.

and fragmentation weapons that were introduced posed greater threats to travelers, but few were capable of causing serious damage to vehicular traffic. Laser-guided weapons could be countered by starting fires to obscure targets with smoke and distract infrared targeting equipment. From May 1968, some of the *Igloo White* sensors were booby-trapped to discourage sappers from removing or disassembling them.

Of all the aerial threats, B-52 *Arc Light* attacks were the most feared. Unseen and unheard at 32,000ft altitude, a three-aircraft cell dropped up to 324 500lb bombs on a mile-long strip of land by 300ft wide, leaving 30ft-wide craters roughly 50ft apart and up to 30ft deep. Other aircraft in a B-52 target area were given a five-minute warning on the Guard radio channel before the stream of bombs began to tear up the jungle. Where they fell, there was total destruction of the forest and any structures or travelers within it. The shock effects could permanently deafen people over half a mile away and anyone caught in the blast at that distance would be rendered unconscious. Survivors suffered from psychological damage for many years. One Viet Cong account of a raid described how a visiting party of Soviet military advisers lost control of their bodily functions during a raid and shook uncontrollably for some hours afterwards. Even the reinforced bunkers along the Trail for those near enough to enter them could not withstand the blast from bombs falling within 2,000ft. Craters filled with water and in lowland, swampy areas, they became invisible beneath the water, drowning any heavily laden troops who inadvertently waded into them. Sometimes, military leaders on the Trail would receive warning that an *Arc Light* raid was imminent, relayed initially from Soviet spy trawlers off the island of Guam, where most B-52s were based, and then passed along the NVA intelligence network with calculations on the likely targets. Occupants of the Trail could then try to take to emergency routes leading away from the area at risk.

US FAC and gunship crews were often impressed by the bravery of truck drivers who continued their journeys while under air attack and refused to abandon their vehicles. Drivers also learned that the best times to travel were at dusk before the gunships arrived and just before sunrise. As daylight broke, they would seek sheltered parks to avoid the daytime bomber missions.

A measure of the strength of North Vietnam's morale might be gained from the comparative failure of the US policy of regularly dropping Chieu Hoi surrender leaflets from O-2, C-47, and other aircraft over the Trail in the hope of persuading the travelers to escape the hardship, sickness, and danger of their task by surrendering. It was an integral part of President Johnson's policy of securing South Vietnam's political integrity by negotiation rather than military force, and some travelers did desert, particularly after sustained exposure to *Arc Light* attacks. But US propaganda underestimated the strength of the North's patriotism and devotion to its leadership, and the power of commanders who forbade their charges to read the leaflets. Disillusionment did spread among many troops when they reached South Vietnam and found that they were not universally welcomed by the local people as they had been promised. In January 1966, 1,600 Viet Cong did defect, using the leaflets to guarantee safe conduct.

The end of Operation *Rolling Thunder* on March 31, 1968 allowed more US strike forces to be diverted to Laos. Areas of the Trails at border crossings were heavily bombed, destroying parts of the roads and forcing the Group 559 laborers to establish many bypasses and access roads from the main routes to rest and supply areas. However, bomb damage of unpaved roads could be repaired quickly by the large workforce, often with the aid of bulldozers. Where the routes passed through the Mu Gia Pass, heavy attacks by B-52s were often used to try and collapse sections of hills and mountains onto the roads, as well as breaking up the paved surfaces. Group 559 laborers usually had the routes cleared and operational again within a couple of days.

The Group's headquarters, moved frequently and never detected by American forces, were established at various locations in Laos within tunnel complexes that were equipped with

The weighty burdens attached to bicycles were a tribute to their manufacturers and to the porters who devised such ingenious methods of steering them. (US Army)

electricity, office facilities, and telephones. From 1966, Group 559 built a series of bases, or Binh Trams, at intervals of roughly 70 miles along the Trails as army centers for rest and medical care. They provided communication facilities to coordinate movements along the routes. Seven were in place by February 1966, rising to 30 by 1970. Throughout this period, North Vietnamese expansion was made possible partly because Hanoi took advantage of the lack of coherent, united government in Laos and also of the United States' reluctance to allow their covert military efforts in a neutral country to be made public or to contravene the Geneva Accords. Hanoi ignored that neutrality, keeping troops in northern Laos and manipulating a situation in which it could play China and the Soviet Union off against each other to gain military support.

North Vietnamese Army strength in Laos increased steadily with around 12,850 troops in place by late 1968 out of a total of 51,500 Pathet Lao and NVA in 144 infantry battalions, with 33 combat support battalions including several with dissident neutralist tribal members.

By 1973, 13 new North Vietnamese People's Air Force (VPAF) airfields had been constructed inside South Vietnam from which air defense could be provided for the Trails, including attempts to intercept *Arc Light* B-52 missions. Helicopters were used throughout the war, transporting supplies at night and evading US attacks, particularly in the Tchepone area.

Dvina and Strela

Soviet supplies of ground-to-air missiles to North Vietnam were limited to the SA-2 from 1965 until 1972, when the SA-7 Strela became available. Mobile SA-2 batteries were reported in southern Laos from July 1971 and the Spectre gunships and B-52s were their primary targets. The first launch at an AC-130 occurred near Tchepone and the pilot managed to evade it with some strenuous split-S maneuvers which over-stressed the wings. All AC-130s then carried up to four radar-jamming pods and radar homing and warning (RHAW) gear. After two more SA-2s were fired at AC-130s in January 1972, the aircraft were provided with Wild Weasel fighter escort carrying anti-radiation missiles as NVA attempts to shoot down an AC-130E with the "big gun" became more intense. Gunship crews became aware of the increasing accuracy of the AAA, as more SON-9A radar directors and PUAZO-5A rangefinders were shipped into Laos for use by the batteries of heavier guns. However, the NVA never destroyed the two automatic TACAN stations in Laos that enabled US aircraft to navigate so accurately.

Training AAA gunners, using basic target models. Pilots often graded gunners from 1 to 9 for accuracy and persistence. Briefings included specific warnings about the better exponents. When skilled "level 9" gunners occupied the same site for some time, they became targets themselves. (Dr. Istvan Toperczer)

Although the SA-7 was a much smaller weapon, fired from a launcher on an infantryman's shoulder and guided by infrared energy, it proved deadly in the North's Easter Offensive in 1972. Numerous South Vietnamese Air Force (SVAF) A-1 Skyraiders together with O-2 and OV-10 anti-insurgency aircraft were downed, and in June an AC-130A (55-0043) was shot down. A Strela fired from the A Shau Valley was initially decoyed by a defensive flare but it broke lock and resumed its lethal journey to the gunship's engine No.3.

Spring offensive

After the drawdown of US forces in 1970, the North Vietnamese were able to upgrade their military capability and continue to improve the Trail roads ready for a major assault on South Vietnam in the spring of 1972. Massive infantry forces entered the country from the DMZ, Cambodia, and Laos, and large-scale battles with ARVN forces occurred around key cities like An Loc. For the first time, armored vehicles were used openly. American airpower was crucial in preventing major ARVN retreats under determined and well-organized NVA attacks. AC-130 gunships were a crucial element, destroying numerous T-54 tanks and mobile AAA units, and causing heavy casualties among the NVA battalions when they were exposed in open ground and daylight. Every NVA assault was eventually beaten back, with very heavy casualties. It was clear that the NVA forces were more effective in defensive and guerrilla situations, and very much at risk from air attack despite improved AAA defenses.

CAMPAIGN OBJECTIVES
Cutting the Trail

The end of French colonial rule in Vietnam left America with the responsibility of supporting an insecure Saigon regime militarily. Initially, only low-key air support using obsolescent equipment was allowed. Forgotten tactics from World War II and Korea had to be relearned using piston-engine aircraft to deliver napalm, flares, and strafing. Four *Farm Gate* B-26 Invaders (redesignated "RB-26" to comply with the Laotian sensitivities) and eight T-28Bs of the 4400th Combat Crew Training Squadron (CCTS) were used in 1961 to train VNAF crews. The RB-26s were withdrawn in 1964 after loss of two aircraft with wing fatigue failure. Remanufactured, strengthened B-26s as A-26A Invaders with more ordnance pylons, increased fuel capacity, and more powerful R-2800-103W engines replaced them.

Operated alongside T-28 Zorros of the 609th SOS, 56th SOW at Nakhon Phanom RTAFB, Thailand, from 1966 they pioneered the night interdiction missions over the Trails which became fundamental to US strategy. Using tactics developed during the Korean War, they flew hazardous, low-altitude "Nimrod" missions over North Vietnam, Laos, and Cambodia, attacking transport, troop concentrations, and supply depots. Cruising at 6,000–7,000ft, a Nimrod was given a target and FAC by a C-130 ABCCC, often based on road-watch data, or flew a night visual reconnaissance mission to locate its own targets. Flying at a shallow bank angle parallel to a road so that he could see downwards, the pilot would turn if he saw trucks, align the target with the lower edge of his engine nacelle, and dive at 25–35 degrees, releasing ordnance at spaced intervals at around 3,500ft.

A second run, possibly a flak suppression strafing attack at 2,000ft, would be made at 90 degrees to the first. Pairs of Nimrods could make coordinated flak attacks with one aircraft drawing the fire while another attacked the gunners from a different angle. Pilots indicated their positions and directions to a FAC by using geographical references to US cities (e.g. "I'm going from Chicago to Miami") rather than compass headings, because the NVA was monitoring their UHF conversations.

A 433rd TFS F-4D overflies the "Dog's Head" choke point and river crossing on the Trail at Ban Laboy, allegedly the most heavily bombed area on the planet. (USAF)

The A-1's fiercely loyal pilots joked that the aircraft (designed in 1944) completed its entire mission at 140kt including takeoff, 40-degree attack dives, and final approach. On return, they would say, "Fill the oil up and check the gas," swearing that its tough naval airframe could, "take a lickin' and keep on tickin.'" (USAF)

The 609th soon became the most successful truck killers before the arrival of the AC-130s, but its A-26As became increasingly vulnerable as NVA defenses multiplied. By 1969, the 56th SOW, renowned for its teamwork successes, announced that, "Geographical area restrictions evolved from experience [with earlier T-28 missions] have been applied to A-1 and A-26 missions," banning them from the Tchepone, Mu Gia Pass, and Ban Laboy Ford regions. After five losses, the USAF replaced A-26s with jet-powered Martin B-57Bs and the last four Nimrods went home in 1970 having destroyed 4,268 trucks and 201 AAA positions. In the words of Brig Gen Wendell Bevan, 432nd TRW commander, they, "wrote the book on how to kill trucks at night and in the most hostile AAA environment we have ever faced."

Although America's policy towards Hanoi prioritized diplomatic persuasion over coercion following *Rolling Thunder*, its main military objective was preventing invasion of the South by North Vietnam. As President Richard Nixon told the press during the transition from *Rolling Thunder*, "As far as airpower is concerned, let me also say this. As we reduce the number of our forces it is particularly important for us to continue our attacks on the infiltration routes." He was signaling the beginning of Operation *Commando Hunt*, organized in seven phases from October 1968 to March 1972. That campaign absorbed the majority of the US military effort until Nixon resumed the bombing of North Vietnam in 1972's Operation *Linebacker*; his final attempt to force a peace agreement upon Hanoi. Gen Westmoreland's main aspiration was clear from early in the war. He wanted enough troops to cut off the Ho Chi Minh Trail, move into Cambodia, and destroy supply dumps and sanctuaries there before expelling NVA forces from the DMZ. After the humiliation of the well-supplied Viet Cong Tet Offensive, Westmoreland asked for 206,000 extra troops for this counter-offensive, but President Johnson preferred negotiations.

Washington's main objective was then to, "reduce the flow of personnel and materiel into the Republic of Vietnam and Cambodia to the lowest possible level" and to "make the enemy pay an increasingly greater cost for his efforts to dominate Southeast Asia." In 1967,

the Chairman of the Joint Chiefs of Staff told senators that, "Most important in my view is the application of as much force as we possibly can … against the lines of communication in order to destroy, hopefully, and at least disrupt and attrit the flow of supplies to the South." *Commando Hunt* operations were designed to achieve this and by October 10, 1970, it expanded into a fifth phase which was intended to make North Vietnam's goals unsustainable. Like *Rolling Thunder*, it was unable to achieve that end despite causing extensive damage.

The US approach to the use of military power in Vietnam was characterized by the determination to protect the Saigon regime and reluctance (particularly by President Johnson) to make full use of his forces in order to curtail Hanoi's ambitions. For McNamara, the *Igloo White* plan seemed to be a feasible alternative to bombing the North. It would make full use of America's most sophisticated technical innovations and the resultant North Vietnamese casualties would occur well away from the eyes of the world's press. McNamara judged that:

> The barrier may not be fully effective at first, but I believe that it can be made effective in time and that even the threat of it becoming effective can substantially change to our advantage the character of the war. It would hinder enemy efforts, would permit more efficient use of the limited number of friendly troops and would be persuasive evidence both that our sole aim is to protect the South from the North and that we intend to see the job through.

For the US government and public, the enormous cost of *Igloo White*, running at $1.7 billion between 1966 and 1971, including the placement and monitoring of 20,000 sensors in Laos, was a far lesser price than losing many more airmen to North Vietnam's heavy defenses. Implementation of *Commando Hunt* was enabled largely because of the cessation of *Rolling Thunder* on November 1, 1968. Air assets devoted to the bombing campaign could then be redirected to Laotian targets, bringing a three-fold increase in sorties in the first month alone. From 1969 to 1971, *Commando Hunt* became the USAF's most important

During the Korean War, A-26s flew 70 percent of the night tactical strike missions. The 20ft muzzle flash from the eight guns tended to blind the pilot at night. Guns were used mainly for flak suppression, but gunpowder smoke entered the cockpit and made greasy patches on the windshield. Six more guns, removed later, were mounted in the wings. (USAF)

operational activity, although most of it happened secretly, away from the public gaze at a time when anti-war feeling was reaching fever pitch in the USA.

Finding the facts

Gathering intelligence on Trail movements was a primary requirement throughout the campaign and it took many forms. The basic source was conventional or infrared photo-reconnaissance imagery. USAF and USN aircraft usually flew weekly or daily sorties throughout the Trail, recording new features like tracks, bridges, truck parks, or AAA emplacements. From 1969, two 432nd TRW RF-4C Phantoms flew early-morning missions over sections which had been attacked the previous day, hoping to record truck debris before it was removed by workers. Often, they found little evidence, even when gunships had apparently devastated many vehicles. Adequate navigation information to determine exact target coordinates was sometimes lacking and bad weather forced RF-4Cs down to around 4,500ft, increasing the risk from AAA. Reconnaissance also included US Army OV-1 Mohawks patrolling the South Vietnam border with radar and external infrared sensors to detect truck movements along exits into Laos. Radar-equipped US Navy EA-1F "Electric Spads" tracked any low-flying enemy helicopters entering mountain passes with military supplies.

Spads to Sandys

One of the key aircraft in the covert Trail war was the 1945-vintage Douglas A-1 Skyraider. In all, 578 A-1s ("Spads" in naval service) from USN reserves entered USAF service. They also saw extensive VNAF service until 1975, including road reconnaissance missions on the Trail and over Cambodia in joint-South Vietnamese/US operations in April 1970, although USAF advisers were often in the pilots' seats.

The multi-place A-1E version excelled as a search and rescue (SAR) escort and in strike, helicopter escort, and close-support roles, with 8,000lb of ordnance and 20mm guns. The single-seat A-1H and A-1J demonstrated the value of a low-cost, tough striker with long endurance, while USAF planners struggled to evolve a suitable replacement. The possibility of re-opening production was considered. By mid-1966, over 90 percent of the bombing in central Laos had been by F-105s and F-4Cs, but throughout 1967 the piston-engine A-1 Skyraiders, T-28s, and A-26Ks were destroying three times as many trucks as the jets. Gen Westmoreland had to weigh the increasing losses of reciprocating engine aircraft to AAA against the better survival rates of less accurate, costlier supersonic fighters.

While the 56th SOW A-1s could fly solo "self-FAC" sorties for *Barrel Roll*, the A-1s flying two-ship armed reconnaissance missions in *Steel Tiger* required FACs to locate targets. Using TACAN to reach the target area, they dived at 45 degrees, dropping ordnance at around 5,000ft. One aircraft used a flare or napalm to illuminate a target for his wingman's bombs. Their plentiful ordnance allowed repeated passes unless they had to be diverted to tackle AAA threats.

By 1965, the USAF's A-1s were flying some unorthodox missions, including several in conjunction with C-123 *Ranch Hand* sorties to clear forest, including the Viet Cong refuge at Boi Loi Woods (known as "Sherwood Forest") near the Cambodian border. After defoliation spraying by C-123s, followed by 1,200 gallons of fuel oil, Skyraiders dropped napalm to start forest fires. The experiment yielded poor results, partly owing to heavy rain. Skyraiders delivered supplies in empty napalm tanks to beleaguered US outposts and their ability to work in primitive conditions was shown by Maj Bernard F. Fisher's Medal of Honor flight on March 10, 1966.

A Shau was a special forces base for observation of NVA troop movements through a valley into Laos. Fisher's A-1E was among six sent from Pleiku AB to attack 2,000 NVA

troops who were invading the base. They had to fly through intense flak from all sides. On the second pass, former F-104 Starfighter pilot Maj "Jump" Myers' A-1E took heavy flak hits, which forced him to make a wheels-up landing on A Shau's small airstrip. He ran from his blazing Skyraider while Fisher's flight strafed enemy troops who were closing in on him and neutralized an AAA site above the airstrip. Fisher landed on the short, debris-strewn airstrip, requiring two attempts to make a relatively safe landing amidst heavy enemy fire which put 19 holes in the aircraft. He taxied back down the pierced steel plank runway full of jagged holes from mortar hits, stopped, and hauled Myers into the cockpit. Fisher then coaxed the A-1E (52-132649) back into the air, still under heavy enemy fire. His flight's intervention and follow-up attacks enabled almost all the A Shau defenders to be evacuated.

The 6th SOW at Nakhon Phanom operated three A-1 squadrons, initially on *Barrel Roll* missions in northern Laos. By December 1969, they flew more *Steel Tiger* sorties, striking mainly at night amidst prodigious AAA. The 1st ACS flew *Igloo White* "gravel" mining missions over the Trail with OP-2Es, flying in formation with the Neptunes so that the two A-1s could drop mines as the OP-2E dispensed its sensors in one pass. Later, they followed behind the OP-2E to reduce AAA risk. After F-4Ds took over sensor "seeding," the A-1 gravel missions continued. Their targets were marked by FACs with white phosphorus rockets and the mines were ejected from six under-wing containers in steep dives from 9,000ft down to 50ft. Straight-and-level runs at that altitude put A-1s at severe risk from innumerable small arms and losses were heavy.

This A-1H bears three SUU-14A/A dispensers on its outer pylons to dispense Dragontooth bomblets such as CBU-14 or CBU-25. A SUU-11/A gun pod with 7.62mm GAU-2B/A minigun and 1,500 rounds, a rocket pod, and a 100lb "Willie Pete" bomb are on inner pylons. (USAF)

A-1G 132612 from the composite 1st/6th SOS, 14th SOW at Pleiku AB, carrying a documentation camera pod. With the 602nd SOS, it was shot down during its fifth "Firefly" CAS attack pass over northern Laos on January 9, 1970. Capt J. L. Hudson, "Firefly 43," was rescued by a pararescue jumper from a 40th ARRS HH-53C. (USAF)

Bringing them home

US policy was always to recover downed aircrew, whatever the cost or complexity of the attempt. A second Medal of Honor, one of only 12 awarded during the Vietnam War, went to another A-1 pilot, Lt Col William Jones III, commander of the 602nd SOS at Nakhon Phanom. As a "Sandy" search and rescue (SAR) escort pilot for a downed 432nd TRW F-4D crew "Carter 02" in jungle near Dong Hoi, he attacked a 37mm AAA flak trap around the Phantom pilot. Two hits damaged his ejection system and radio and started a fire. Severely burned, he jettisoned his canopy but abandoned an attempt to bail out manually, knowing that he could pinpoint the downed pilot's location for the rescuers. An F-100F Misty crew yelled "Bail out!" Instead, he nursed the badly damaged A-1H for 90 miles to Nakhon Phanom, landed in poor visibility with his windscreen fire-blackened, and insisted on showing base personnel the rescue site on his maps before being carried off to surgery. The F-4D pilot, Capt J. R. Wilson, was rescued later that day. Jones' A-1H, 52-139738 "The Proud American," was repaired and it became the last A-1 to be lost in combat, shot down over northern Laos while covering the evacuation of a medical casualty on September 28, 1972.

A-1 pilots performed many other acts of outstanding courage in covering SAR attempts over Laos and Vietnam. At Nakhon Phanom, six A-1 pilots were usually kept on SAR alert. A SAR flight usually consisted of four A-1s, two HH-3 helicopters (replacing shorter-range Kaman HH-43 Huskies, or "Pedros" which performed a high proportion of the rescue missions during the war and were noted for their ability to hover at low altitude), and an HC-130 ABCCC aircraft. They could orbit a rescue site for up to five hours, under constant threat from ground fire, carrying varied ordnance including specialized smoke bombs to screen a rescue area, "gravel" mines, and CBU-19 tear gas. Strafing in the mountainous karst

landscape of northern Laos was considered too risky, particularly at night, except to relieve beleaguered troops or downed aircrew. By 1967, the Sandy A-1s sustained the highest loss rates for any USAF aircraft in Southeast Asia. Ninety-six of the 266 USAF and USN A-1 losses were over Laos, but they markedly increased the number of successful rescues.

SAR attempts could become major operations involving numerous aircraft over several days. On an armed reconnaissance mission by a Stormy FAC flight including F-4D Phantom II (66-8773) over southern Laos on January 17, 1969, the crew attacked a 37mm AAA site. One F-4D was hit, crashing in flames. The back-seat WSO managed to eject and triggered a rescue effort that involved 284 aircraft. From the first flight of Sandy A-1Hs, one (52-134632) was shot down and an HH-53B helicopter "Jolly Green 67" moved in to rescue its pilot, Lt Col Lurrie Morris, commander of the 602nd SOS, and search for the F-4D crew. It was badly damaged and crash-landed near Tchepone. A second HH-53B "Jolly Green 70" moved in to rescue its crew and Morris while strike aircraft destroyed "Jolly Green 67" to prevent its capture. The following day, as the search for the F-4 pilot continued, another Sandy (52-134588) and its pilot, Capt Robert Coady, were lost to intense 37mm fire. An O-2A, assessing damage to trucks from the previous night, was hit in the same area and the rescue force was diverted to pick up its crew while Sandys kept the enemy away with tear gas.

One of the biggest SAR operations took place in one of the most heavily defended areas of the Trail near Ban Phanop in southern Laos to recover a 12th TFW F-4C crew, "Boxer 22." After a 37mm hit the crew ejected and a 51-hour rescue attempt involving 366 sorties (171 by A-1 Sandys) began on December 5, 1969. On the first day, seven Nakhon Phanom helicopters

Aerial detection of this heavily camouflaged 37mm 61-K gun would have posed considerable problems. The loader holds a five-round clip, while others in the crew of eight aim the gun with its daylight AZP-37 sight. (Dr. Istvan Toperczer)

Successfully managing a SAR often relied on a FAC's skill to coordinate the various airborne elements. A Cessna O-2A "Mixmaster" like this example (67-21436) offered long endurance but its 300lb of avionics and ordnance load of LAU-59/A or MA-2A rocket launchers, flares, logs, and SUU-11 miniguns reduced performance and hampered single-engine flight. (USAF)

attempted a recovery, one of them getting its tail boom stuck in a tree. All were driven away by ground fire and 47 A-1 sorties from all three squadrons were flown around the clock to suppress gunfire from around a hundred sources. The F-4C pilot, Capt Ben Danielson, was killed by NVA troops but his back-seater, 1Lt Woodie Bergeron, was finally snatched by an HH-53 from behind a heavy smokescreen after two nights on the ground or immersed in a river under foliage. A parajumper was killed and five A-1s and 12 other aircraft received severe damage. The A-1 Sandy force of 24 aircraft returned to Nakhon Phanom en masse and 4,000 people at the base turned out to greet the HH-53 containing Bergeron. It was a graphic demonstration of the US objective of protecting its own men at great cost. That knowledge was undoubtedly supportive to airmen as they undertook extraordinarily risky missions over Laos and Vietnam. Many shot-down pilots recalled that the sound of a Sandy overhead lifted their spirits in desperate situations.

Another extraordinary example of the determination of SAR crews occurred on April 2, 1972, when EB-66C 54-0466 "Bat 21," providing ECM protection for an *Arc Light* attack, was shot down by an SA-2 near the DMZ. Only one crew member, 53-year-old navigator Lt Col Iceal "Gene" Hambleton, ejected, landing close to an NVA troop concentration. The largest SAR operation of the war was mounted over the following 11 days. An HC-130 "King Bird" flying over the site was damaged by another SA-2 but a Da Nang-based O-2A FAC, Lt Col Bill Jankowski, contacted Hambleton as he parachuted down. His position was later confirmed by Capt Gary Ferentchak in a Pave Nail OV-10A. Sandy A-1s moved in, strafing NVA troops within 300ft of Hambleton's position. Four US Army helicopters attempted a rescue but two were shot down. Several FACs remained on station the next day, one of them (OV-10A Nail 38) being shot down by an SA-2. Over the following 11 days, 90 strike sorties were flown daily to protect Hambleton and another OV-10A, "Covey 282," was lost. On April 6, in a final rescue effort, a 37th ARRS HH-53C was hit by machine-gun fire and all its occupants were killed when it crashed. Hambleton was eventually able to reach a riverbank, where he was rescued by a special forces SEAL team which had also recovered Nail pilot 1Lt Mark Clark. SEAL team leader Lt Tom Norris was awarded the Medal of Honor for his rescue effort.

For close-in, "bare knuckles" fighting, the A-1 proved to be ideal. Five A-1s were on alert at Nakhon Phanom in 1968 to support SOG surveillance teams in the jungle. The SOG commander, John Singlaub, made an impassioned plea for the A-1 to continue as their tactical air supporter when USAF policy was to phase it out: Seventh AF Commander Gen William Momyer wanted an all-jet air force. Flying at extremely low altitudes, the "Spads" would dodge beneath the yellowish streams of 23mm AAA and the seven-round clips of apparently slow-moving red fireballs from 37mm guns. They often returned with extraordinary structural damage from AAA hits. On one occasion, they were directed to drop ordnance within 60ft of a reconnaissance team that was about to be overrun by NVA troops. They followed up with 20mm strafing a mere 15ft from friendly forces, routing the enemy.

North Vietnamese troops on the Trail, photographed covertly by a Studies and Observation Group (SOG) team. US and Laotian reconnaissance teams were often inserted to monitor enemy activity, but they would in turn be hunted by NVA patrols. (US Army)

From August 1968, 6th SOS A-1s were frequently given truck-hunting missions in southern Laos. They were joined at Nakhon Phanom by the 22nd SOS, whose A-1s had black undersides for nighttime *Steel Tiger* and *Barrel Roll* interdiction. The 602nd SOS sent a detachment to Udorn RTAFB which adopted a "Dragonfly" call-sign for missions over northern Laos, while its "Firefly" A-1s fought in eastern Laos. Its "Sandy" detachment at Nakhon Phanom specialized in search and rescue cover. One mission was to recover 23-year-old MiG-killer Thunderchief pilot 1Lt Karl Richter, shot down on his 198th mission and impaled on a sharp karst mountainside. Sadly, he died of his injuries in the rescue helicopter. The rescue attempt for a USMC OV-10A crew on April 21, 1970, cost three Sandy A-1s but all three pilots were recovered.

Mid-air collisions over targets were a constant hazard at night as the aircraft usually extinguished their formation lights, "going Christmas tree" briefly only to establish visual contact with strike aircraft. A 34th Tactical Group A-1E flown by Capt Robert Gallup struck John Rumph's A-1G during a strike on a VC force threatening a special forces camp on June 16, 1965. Half of Rumph's right wing was removed and Gallup's (52-135040) aircraft crashed, killing him, while Rumph bailed out manually from 52-133889 and took a UH-1 Huey ride home with head injuries.

OPPOSITE TYPICAL RESCUE AND RECOVERY OF A SHOT-DOWN PILOT IN LAOS

On December 8, 1968, Maj Tom O'Connor of the 602nd SOS, 56th SOW at Nakhon Phanom RTAFB was flying A-1J Skyraider 52-142033 as "Firefly 34" on a strike mission close to the abandoned Lima Site 85 radar installation in northern Laos. His aircraft's left wing caught fire after an AAA hit and he bailed out, landing on a steep hillside (1). Two Air America helicopters (2) attempted a rescue but were repulsed by intense ground fire. An HH-3E Jolly Green Giant rescue helicopter with four 602nd SOS "Sandy" A-1s, led by Capt Jerry Jenkinson, and an HC-130P Hercules tanker (3) approached from Nakhon Phanom, with four additional Sandy A-1s led by Maj Palank (3A). F-4 bombers (4) attacked AAA positions ahead of the rescue and suppressed ground fire around the rescue area. The HH-3E lowered its penetrator device to pick up O'Connor but was hit by ground fire. The Sandy force (5) circled his position, hitting Pathet Lao troops within a few hundred feet of O'Connor. Capt James Miers' HH-53 "Super Jolly" (6) moved in, O'Connor fired his last Mk 13 orange smoke flare, and the penetrator was lowered to pick him up. The HH-53 withdrew to make a refuel from the HC-130P. Another RESCAP A-1J (52-142035, Sandy 6) was lost during the rescue, probably stalling while strafing (7). Capt Joe Pirrucello was unable to eject before the aircraft crashed into a mountain.

B-57B Canberras were camouflaged from December 1965. FACs praised their bombing accuracy. The two-man crew, a big wing giving considerable maneuverability, and its relatively quiet engines made it ideal for single-aircraft interdiction. The 8th (PQ codes) and 13th BS (PV) moved to Phan Rang AB in October 1966 for the rest of the war. (USAF)

Introducing jets

RF-101 and RB-57 reconnaissance jet aircraft were active over Laos from 1964 and B-57B Canberras were deployed to South Vietnam from August 1964 in response to the imminent collapse of the Saigon regime. They flew Trail missions for over seven years. The 1954 Geneva Accords specified that only propeller-driven aircraft could be used and no "new military weaponry" was allowed, but it was felt by 1964 that the presence of jet bombers would subdue the enemy's ambitions. Unable to commit its forces directly unless "provoked," Washington used the Gulf of Tonkin Incident as a pretext to redeploy the B-57Bs of the Japan-based 3rd BW (the USAF's last Tactical Bombardment Wing, scheduled for deactivation in 1964) to Bien Hoa AB. They performed a limited number of unarmed road reconnaissance missions in South Vietnam until February 1965, when attacks in both South and North Vietnam were

sanctioned. B-57B 53-3888 made the first live ordnance attack by a US jet bomber against an enemy target on February 19, 1965, and more missions followed in which the B-57 crews gained a reputation for accuracy. It was a turning point in the campaign. Rather than scaling down the US effort, Washington began to discuss further troop deployments to end the war decisively.

Their success in these tasks led to Trail missions from March 1965 with one B-57B to drop flares, illuminating a target for a second aircraft. Missions were also flown in collaboration with the 609th SOS A-26As and C-130 Blind Bat flare-ships, using USMC EF-10B Skyknight ECM aircraft of VMCJ-1 to jam enemy radars. Two B-57Bs flew close to the C-130 at 8,000ft, looking for the lights of a truck convoy. B-57Bs started to descend as the Blind Bat released parachute flares over targets. If trucks attempted to escape, attacks were then made beside the roads next to their last known location and several were usually hit. A "Patricia Lynn" RB-57E, equipped for night photography, could then follow up the strike.

The first night mission over Laos, flown by two 8th BS B-57Bs led by Capt Ben Stone, occurred near Tchepone on April 1, 1965, beginning Operation *Steel Tiger*. Four trucks on a ferry and one bridge were destroyed. For their few "Doom Pussy" night interdictions into North Vietnam, B-57Bs carried their own Mk 24 flares. The loss of ten B-57Bs and 27 personnel in a catastrophic flight-line explosion on May 16, 1965, at Bien Hoa was a disaster for the 3rd BW. Thirteen bombs (one of them wrongly fused) loaded on the "Jade" flight B-57B manned by Capts C. N. Fox and V. L. Haynes exploded as it started its engines. Thirty A-1 Skyraiders were also damaged and one was destroyed in this, the USAF's worst accident of the war. Five more B-57s were lost to Viet Cong mortar attacks, so two Air National Guard units had to surrender aircraft as replacements, but B-57B operations began to wind down in 1968.

On March 15, 1966, Capt Larry Mason's B-57B was hit while strafing trucks near Tchepone. He became the first living aviator to receive the Air Force Cross after returning

Two "Black Spot" NC-123Ks were modified by E-Systems as part of *Shed Light* for night interdiction. After operational tests over Laos and Korea, they were redesignated AC-123Ks in 1969. (USAF)

the badly damaged aircraft to Da Nang, thereby saving the life of his wounded navigator. Although large areas of the right wing were destroyed by AAA, the aircraft was returned to action and later remanufactured as a B-57G.

Big stick strategy

After the defeat of the Viet Cong in the battles of the Tet Offensive, the defense of the Trail was controlled by professional NVA troops and ever-increasing numbers of AAA weapons. However, the prospect of mass destruction of large areas of the Trail and its traffic, even in a supposedly neutral country, suggested that the campaign might be shortened by such hammer blows. TF Alpha and Seventh AF agreed a list of 53 crucial targets (listed as "truck parks") that could theoretically be obliterated by B-52s, guided by Combat Skyspot radar positions on the ground.

Operation *Turnpike*, from April 19 to June 24, 1968, included B-52s and tactical aircraft in a major program of attacks, focused on the Mu Gia and Ban Karai Passes. Although poor weather and forest cover made the results hard to assess, the available sensor data indicated that traffic had been reduced by rockfall damage and blockages in the passes, and by destruction of the truck parks at the head of the routes into Laos. All B-52 attacks required approval from the US Ambassador in Vientiane and they had to be directed into target "boxes" that were already agreed with him.

Campaign priorities

From World War II onwards, the USAF had done little to develop night-attack capability and this became a real handicap during the Trail campaign, requiring Project *Shed Light* to develop solutions. In 1966, the most credible aircraft for the purpose were the US Army's side-looking radar (SLAR) and infrared (IR) equipped OV-1 Mohawks. USAF F-102A interceptors were employed briefly, using their IR sensors and missiles to detect and attack Trail traffic. In 1966, the US Navy Grumman S-2D Tracker was chosen as a USAF night-attack prototype for use from 1968, but it was soon rejected as being too slow. The Air Staff wanted to accelerate *Shed Light*, and the summer of 1968 Air Force Systems Command was belatedly developing 100 projects to bring technical innovation to the burgeoning war on trucks. By 1969, Trails traffic had increased to the point where technology was increasingly called upon to provide self-contained attack aircraft which could detect, mark, and attack their targets. This was intended to lead eventually to the ultimate goal of operating the General Dynamics F-111D Aardvark as an all-weather striker that could find its own targets.

Interim projects included a B-26K fitted with an experimental, forward-looking infrared (FLIR) unit. Four A-1E Skyraiders were tested with massive Dalmo Victor Corporation low light level television (LLLTV) pods beneath their left wings in January 1968 in Project *Tropic Moon I*. The pods' cameras provided wide and narrow (search) angle views to survey roads in light equating to a quarter-moon minimum in clear weather without haze or smoke, but the sensitive cameras were burned out by sudden bursts of light from rockets or flares.

Transferred to Nakhon Phanom, four of the A-1Es, with black undersides, flew straight-and-level Zorro missions in southern Laos with the 602nd SOS. They carried flares to illuminate attacks with napalm, bombs, or CBU once targets had been identified with the LLLTV which, in ideal conditions, allowed them to see unlighted targets at around two miles. Like other attackers, they tried to hit the first and last vehicles in a convoy so that the rest could be trapped for later attack. Trucks had their headlights shuttered to mere slits but these could be seen by LLLTV from the front elevation. By the end of their deployment on November 30, 1968, the aircraft, Zorro 51 to 54, had flown many Trails missions, sustaining only superficial damage and achieving successes against convoys, troops, and barge traffic

An A-6C TRIM of VA-145 "Swordsmen" in 1971. The large underbelly fairing for the RCA LLLTV and Texas Instruments FLIR equipment slowed the aircraft on catapult launch but added stability on landing. TRIM equipment was also installed in four of VAH-21's AP-2H Neptunes, with guns and 40mm grenade launchers for Trail operations. (US Navy)

between Laos and Cambodia. The *Tropic Moon I* equipment was fairly primitive, but it proved that LLLTV was a way of penetrating the night.

The success of the 3rd BW B-57Bs as truck hunters prompted *Tropic Moon II*. Three Phan Rang-based B-57Bs were equipped with Westinghouse LLLTV pods under their left wings in December 1957, together with a laser rangefinder and a weapons-delivery computer. In an eight-month operational test 456 trucks were detected, but only 39 were hit, as they could not be identified early enough with the narrow-range radar to make first-pass attacks. Tests in the Mekong Delta were curtailed after a police station was accidentally hit. The aircraft were transferred to the *Tiger Hound* area.

In 1969, 16 Phan Rang aircraft were more heavily modified as B-57G night interdiction aircraft in *Tropic Moon III*, costing $49m per aircraft. A new Martin-built nose section contained a Westinghouse sensor suite, comprising a forward-looking radar with a moving target indicator (MTI) that could detect a jeep at eight miles, LLLTV, an infrared detector, explosion-proofed fuel tanks, and a new bombing computer. A laser target marker for LGBs was also fitted and all the sensors and ECM were controlled from the rear cockpit. Targets were detected with the forward-looking radar and MTI, and identified with LLLTV. For LGB delivery they were marked with the laser and four Mk 82 Pave Way I bombs could then be dropped accurately on a heat source or TV-identified location. In the bomb-bay, a Hayes modular bomb dispenser contained M36s with BLU-26 bomblets. Air Staff planned combined operations by B-57Gs and AC-130s that would "reduce North Vietnam's truck inventory by 40 to 50 percent of its present level in six months of operations."

Issued to the 13th Bomb Squadron (Tactical) under Lt Col Paul Pitt, the B-57Gs moved to Ubon RTAFB in October 1970 (a year late) under *Coronet Condor* for 18 months of combat, following 37 months of extended delays and equipment shortcomings. The 11 aircraft often rivalled AC-130s for truck kills and greatly exceeded results by fighters. By January 15, 1971, they had sighted 759 trucks and destroyed 363. However, delays, cost overruns, and failures in refining their sensors caused tremendous maintenance and availability problems (averaging 56 man-hours per flight hour) up to their withdrawal in the spring of 1972. The MTI never worked efficiently and the forward-looking radar was

unreliable owing to weak magnetrons. Also, AAA forced the aircraft to fly at inappropriate altitudes for their sensors.

Related projects included Pave Gat, in which a B-57G was tested with a downward-firing M61A1 Vulcan gun in an Emerson turret, slaved to the electro-optical sensor. It could destroy three times as many trucks as bombs did and it kept the aircraft away from flak. Excess costs

B-57G 53-3865 of the 13th TBS, 8th TFW at Ubon in December 1970 ahead of another night on the Trail. It was the first USAF bomber designed for self-contained night attacks. When targets were identified, four external Mk 82 Pave Way Is, 750lb GP bombs, and M35 or M36 firebombs were delivered with 80 percent accuracy. (USAF)

An AC-47D pilot had a Mk 20 Mod 4 gunsight in the left cockpit side-window and a trigger button on his control wheel. The six-man crew included three gun mechanics. The forward three fuselage windows had ballistic cloth armor to deflect small-arms fire from the storage area for 24,000 rounds of ammunition and 45 flares. A smoke extractor protruded from the third window. (USAF)

O-1 FAC pilots orbited targets at around 85kt, above 1,500ft, searching for targets through binoculars and marking them with white phosphorus "Willie Pete" rockets. Strike aircraft could attack only when "cleared hot" by a FAC. Any "friendly" casualties owing to inaccurate bombing were the FAC's responsibility. Only two shot-down O-1 FACs were rescued in Laos in 1966–67 and 12 were never found. No "Raven" pilots were recovered. (USAF)

and the imminent departure of the aircraft from Thailand denied Pave Gat any operational testing. Another project equipped a B-57B with no fewer than 52 downward-firing M60C guns in its bomb-bay.

The B-57G was a small-scale, expensive addition to the Trail campaign, but it pioneered technology for later combat aircraft and replaced Blind Bat C-130s in June 1970. As Secretary of the Air Force, Robert Seamans hoped, they generated "lessons which would be valuable in developing similar systems for the future."

Similar sensors used in the Grumman A-6C Intruder showed that the night interdiction campaign could be improved if sufficient funding was allocated for the technology. However, LLLTV was ineffective for most of the monsoon periods, when trucks could often move with impunity. Between March 6 and September 25, CIA road-watch teams reported sightings of 11,712 trucks, but only 101 were destroyed.

One B-57G (53-3931) was lost. Lt Col Pitt and squadron sensor officer Lt Col Ed Buschette crashed during a nocturnal Trail mission, having apparently collided with O-2A Nail FAC 67-21428. Both crew members of the FAC aircraft suffered the fate of many in Laos. Although at least one ejected, they were never seen again. Pitt and Buschette were rescued near the DMZ and the aircraft's remains were napalmed to preserve its many secrets.

A B-57E (55-4284) collided with a "Candlestick" flare-dropping C-123K on a December 13, 1968, *Steel Tiger* mission. The C-123K crew were using their Starlight scope to find targets for two B-57Es south of the Ban Karai Pass. As it made its bomb run, Maj Wayne Dugan's Canberra hit the C-123 and crashed, killing both crew. Six of the C-123K crew bailed out as their aircraft spun downwards, but the only survivor was the pilot, Lt T. M. Turner, who was knocked unconscious and bailed out later. It was a bad night for the nocturnal strikers,

with another mid-air collision that destroyed an AC-47D and an OV-10A FAC, killing the crew of the latter.

Flexible strategies

Military policies and requirements engendered adaptability for existing equipment. Nuclear strike fighters flew in World War II-type formations to attack cities as strategic bombers in Operation *Rolling Thunder*, while B-52 strategic bombers often became close-support tactical aircraft. On a smaller scale, US Navy anti-submarine patrollers served as sensor-droppers over the forests of Laos for the Trail Road Interdiction Mission (TRIM) role, diving and weaving like fighters as they tried to avoid ground fire. F-4 Phantom supersonic interceptors became sensor-droppers, forward air control platforms, and level bombers in MSQ-77 radar bombing formations.

Faced with an unexpectedly resilient and resourceful enemy force, the USA had to devise innovative strategies. Some of those responses involved the most advanced technology that US scientists could offer, such as LLLTV and laser targeting. Many others involved elderly military equipment combined with basic human ingenuity and courage. Typifying the latter, Airman John Lee Levitov was loadmaster on AC-47 "Spooky 71" (tailcode EN 770) on February 24, 1969, during a night attack on Long Binh US Army base. The AC-47 established its pylon turn over the base while Levitov was setting up Mk 24 target-illuminating flares and passing them to the gunners to drop. Each 27lb magnesium flare developed two million candlepower, burning at 4,000 degrees Fahrenheit for three minutes. Orbiting at low altitude, the aircraft was hit by a stray Viet Cong 82mm mortar, which tore a 2ft hole in the wing and

The "Big Belly" modification enabled B-52Ds to carry three pre-loaded B-Bay high-density bomb-racks internally, each one holding 28 Mk 82 500lb bombs. Another 24 were hung on the under-wing racks for a total of 108 weapons, or 66 750lb M117 bombs. (USAF)

penetrated the fuselage in 3,500 places. All the occupants of the main fuselage were injured and the gunner fell over, dropping the activated flare he was holding, which would have destroyed the aircraft if it had fully ignited.

Levitov, although wounded in 40 places by shrapnel, moved an injured crewman away from the open loading door and tried to pick up the smoking flare, which was rolling around on the floor as the pilot tried to regain control of the aircraft. Levitov's Medal of Honor citation stated that he struggled forward despite the loss of blood from his many wounds and partial loss of feeling in his right leg. Unable to grasp the rolling flare with his hands, he threw himself bodily upon it. Hugging the deadly device to his body, he dragged himself back to the rear of the aircraft and hurled the flare through the open cargo door. At that instant, the flare separated and ignited in the air, but clear of the aircraft. Sgt Levitov, by his selfless and heroic actions, saved the aircraft and the entire crew from certain death and destruction.

In some ways, the most important contributors to the *Commando Hunt* interdiction strikes, which extended from the "dry" season of 1968–69 until the spring of 1972, were the slow, fragile Cessna O-1 (orbiting at 85mph and suffering many engine failures and inadequate nighttime instrumentation) and O-2A FAC aircraft. Both carried seven-shot "Willie Pete" (white phosphorus) marker rocket pods which were also used to attack trucks in daylight, or to keep hostile heads down as the FAC awaited a strike flight. The O-2A's twin "push-pull" engine arrangement provided better safety but, like many US aircraft, the fuel tanks were vulnerable to small-arms fire. FACs grew accustomed to seeing rifle fire like a series of flashbulbs going off, as they flew within a few hundred feet of enemy locations to launch their marker rockets or dropped marker "logs" ahead of a convoy and out of the drivers' sight. A flare could be dropped upwind of the target to illuminate it and the navigator then identified it with binoculars, ready for a marker rocket launch. The pilot then entered an orbit to the side of the strikers' approach headings and remained to give bomb damage assessment in which burning trucks were counted as "kills."

Cambodia

US policy towards Prince Norodom Sihanouk's government in Cambodia took advantage of his ambivalent position. Lacking the military strength to oppose North Vietnamese use of his territory for parts of the Trail, he also secretly connived at US bombing of those occupied areas. Initially, those missions were recorded as being over South Vietnam, but the Operation *Menu* B-52 missions into Cambodia from 1969 against the North Vietnamese logistical installations required a complex tissue of deception to avoid escalating the anti-war movement in the USA. *Menu* failed to force Hanoi into negotiation and the policy of "Vietnamization," designed to allow the USA to escape from Vietnam, was fatally damaged by the invasion of Cambodia in Operation *Lam Son 719* in 1971, in which North Vietnamese forces decimated the South Vietnamese regiments. Pentagon experts proposed to revitalize Vietnamization by arming VNAF Skyraiders with powerful CBU-55 fuel-air explosives and supplying mini-gunship Helio Stallion lightplanes with single sideways-firing 20mm rotary cannon to take on Trail missions in Operation *Commando Hunt VII*, rather than handing over sophisticated AC-130s and relying on B-52s and *Igloo White*.

Although Washington was reluctant to risk its primary nuclear deterrent over North Vietnamese long-range defenses, confining most B-52 missions to South Vietnam, B-52s played an increasing role in the Trail war in 1971. *Commando Hunt VII* included extensive *Arc Light* attacks to block the mountain passes from South Vietnam into Laos, isolating traffic which could no longer be attacked in North Vietnam. Passes leading from North Vietnam were avoided because of SA-2 missiles. After Operation *Linebacker II*, huge quantities of weapons and 40,000 additional NVA troops were moved down the Trail, but President Nixon did not respond with punitive bombing there or in North Vietnam. Instead, bombing was

resumed in Cambodia to support the Phnom Penh regime, under attack by Khmer Rouge forces. Thailand-based tactical units and B-52s began intensive bombing until Congress halted it on August 15, 1973, ending the longest aerial campaign in history.

LORAN-D-equipped F-4D-33-MC 66-8803 of the 497th TFS "Night Owls" at Ubon with black undersides, Mk 82 bombs, and M36 "funny" bombs for truck attacks. CBU-2 (BLU-3 fragmentation bombs in a rear-firing SUU-7 dispenser) was available for low-altitude, straight-and-level attacks but SUU-7s sometimes damaged the F-4s' wings. (USAF)

Intruders on the Trail

During 1968, the rules of engagement for Trail attacks were loosened to reduce delays between the detection of trucks and subsequent attacks. Napalm was allowed and armed reconnaissance pilots could attack targets of opportunity without the presence of a FAC. By 1969, radar and LORAN-directed bombing was allowed generally and the US Navy's TRIM-equipped A-6C Intruders with radar systems that included a moving target indicator for truck attacks were permitted to operate independently on night armed reconnaissance missions. Those aircraft entered combat with VA-165 "Boomers" in 1970 and flew 675 combat missions against Trail traffic in *Commando Bolt* and *Commando Nail* operations, finding that the LLLTV worked well in moonlight and daylight, while the FLIR was too difficult to focus in combat conditions. Only 7 percent of the Boomers' sorties actually used the sensors, mainly because of the monsoon weather.

Later cruises with VA-145 yielded better results. A-6Cs received a laser target marker in place of LLLTV and an improved FLIR gave VA-35 "Panthers" a chance to demonstrate the aircraft's accuracy with Mk 82 Pave Way I laser-guided bombs in 1972. Sophisticated electronics were no guarantee of surviving the concentrated defenses around choke points or narrow passes, where the aircraft had little choice about the direction of their attacks. VA-196 lost two A-6As to AAA within two days in December 1968 while attacking *Steel Tiger* targets near the A Shau Valley in Laos. VA-165, impeded by shortages of aircraft and spares, could claim only 14 trucks for a monthly expenditure of 3,858 bombs.

USN A-6s were valued for *Steel Tiger* and *Tiger Hound* operations after *Rolling Thunder*. Major traffic bottlenecks, at Ha Tinh and Phu Dien Chau, came within the Strike Package

Preparing to live up to its nickname, this Skyraider bears M117s, "Daisy Cutter" Mk 81s, and rocket pods. The 2,700hp R-3350-26WA engine shed much of its 39 gallons of oil, necessitating regular wash-downs. Oil on the wings made nighttime maintenance and crew entry slippery tasks, sticking to boots and suits, and sometimes causing a fall off the wing. (USAF)

areas allotted to the USN, and over 600 trucks were destroyed there by November 1968. The A-6's unique night-attack capability was superior to anything the USAF could muster in quantity at the time. As VA-196 bombardier/navigator Stan Walker recalled,

the A-6 was at its best during night armed reconnaissance (ARREC) because of the moving target indicator capability. We often carried six CBU-24s on these missions. They were very effective because a drop using two could cover a very large area. Any reasonably accurate bombing solution would usually result in ground fires which could then be bombed visually by 'pouncer' bombers such as the A-7A Corsair II, following the A-6. Later in the 1968 cruise we usually took an A-7 as wingman. We would search, acquire a target, bomb it and select 'flares' immediately so that eight seconds later a Mk 24 flare would launch from a SUU-40 pod to light the target for the A-7. It was impossible to actually see a convoy of trucks until they were hit at night. I recall having a string of seven trucks burning from a single drop.

USMC aircraft also flew classified *Steel Tiger* missions, many of them night sorties by Chu Lai-based F-4s reducing the AAA defenses on entrances to the Trail, particularly in the A Shau Valley. Mk 82 bombs with "Daisy Cutter" fuse extensions or 12-hour delayed fuses were often dropped. The flak multiplied and by June 1969 VMFA-334 Red Devils F-4J pilots were reporting target areas "ablaze with muzzle flashes" during *Steel Tiger* bombing runs. Their AN/APR-25 radar warning scopes revealed AAA radars that were tracking the Phantoms, each one being shown as a line on the scope indicating the direction of the emitter from aircraft. On some missions, the "triple A" was so heavy that pilots would turn off their AN/APR-25 scopes to minimize distraction on their bomb runs.

THE CAMPAIGN
Steel Tiger and *Barrel Roll*

Bombing the Laotian Trail network began on March 21, 1965, and two areas were identified for attack. Targets in the southern panhandle area were included in the *Steel Tiger* program. Those in northern Laos came under Operation *Barrel Roll*, where USAF FAC pilots often worked with Laotian T-28s striking Pathet Lao forces. An indigenous crew member was added for sorties to count as "training exercises" within the rules of engagement, although *Barrel Roll* operations were often complicated by language difficulties. By June 1965, over 4,000 *Steel Tiger* sorties had been flown, rising to 8,000 in January 1966. Strikes by tactical aircraft controlled by FACs accounted for most of the truck-killing missions up to 1968.

FAC pilots in Cessna O-1 Bird Dogs and O-2A Skymasters ("Oscar 2s") of the 20th TASS "Coveys" at Da Nang with 37th ARRS rescue helicopters and 56th SOW A-1 Skyraiders, or 23rd TASS "Nails" based at Nakhon Phanom RTAFB were the vital directors of airstrikes on the Trail and became priority targets for the enemy. Nail O-2A pilots, flying in the Operation *Cricket West* target area within *Barrel Roll* and *Steel Tiger* territory and cruising at 110kt with a Royal Lao Army observer aboard, knew that they had $10,000 bounties on their heads. As well as plotting infiltration routes and directing strike fighters to targets, they could use their own guns and 2.75in. HEI rocket armament to participate in attacks on troops or AAA sites. Their only defenses in hostile airspace were close knowledge of the terrain and its hazards; "jinking," slight, random course changes every ten seconds to present a difficult target for gunners; "cross-controlling;" and using the rudders to induce uncoordinated flight. At low altitudes, they often fought at much closer quarters than most tactical pilots. A 21st TASS O-1G pilot, Capt Hilliard Wilbanks, was posthumously awarded the Medal of Honor for preventing an ARVN battalion from entering a Viet Cong ambush on February 24, 1967. On his 488th combat mission, he supervised attacks by Army helicopters and F-4s to hold back superior VC forces, finally resorting to treetop passes, firing his automatic rifle from his cockpit window. After three low-level passes, his Bird Dog was finally shot down and he was fatally injured. An O-2A Nail FAC, Maj Gerald T. Dwyer, was hit by 37mm flak over troops on the Trail on May 21, 1968. He bailed out and evaded five heavily armed soldiers,

Cartridge starter smoke streams from a napalm-laden 8th BS B-457B at Da Nang in 1965. These aircraft, at war for five-and-a-half years, carried 20mm or .50-cal guns, but the favored Trail ordnance was the M36E2 "funny bomb" or BLU-27 napalm and 750lb M117 bombs. (USAF)

Col Leroy Manor, 37th TFW commander and a great "Misty" proponent, prepares for a mission, with Col Malcolm Horton in the back of F-100F 56-3874. (Author's Collection)

shooting three and bringing in an airstrike to eliminate the other two before he was rescued by helicopter.

At low altitudes but higher speeds, 155 Misty FAC pilots in two-seat F-100Fs flew "Fast FAC" missions from June 1967 over areas of the Trail where heavy defenses ruled out slower FAC aircraft. In former Misty pilot Gen Don Shepperd's opinion, this was probably the most exciting flying a fighter pilot could find in Vietnam. They detected troops and supply dumps, often calling in F-100Ds to attack them. Capt Jim Brasier, with the 306th TFS in 1968, took off with Lt Mack Sennett in response to a Misty report of a convoy heading south.

We quickly loaded the "Huns" with two LAU-3 rocket pods and two 750lb bombs and headed north. We contacted Misty and he briefed us on the situation. It was unusual for a convoy to be traveling during the day. A flight of F-100s were pulling off the target and I could see trucks burning through the murky under-cast. Misty put in a Willy Pete rocket to mark our target and cleared us in "hot." On the first pass, I was going to fire my rockets at the head of the convoy and Mack was going to fire at the rear. I rolled in and I could barely make out the flames of a couple of burning trucks. It was still bright sunshine above the under-cast but as I entered the murk in a 30 degree dive it instantly turned to a hazy, smoky night-time and my only point of reference was the burning trucks. I put the [gunsight] pipper on the lead truck, fired both pods of rockets and started my 4g pull-out. As I reached level flight there was a long burst of 23mm or 37mm tracer rounds fired from my left, just in front of my aircraft. There must have been at least 1,000 rounds heading almost horizontally across the sky. I knew I was dead, or had been hit. I instinctively pulled as many Gs as the Hun would take. I checked the gauges, but there were no fire lights or smoke – I just couldn't figure out why my jet wasn't hit. I must have entered a valley with mountains where the AAA was coming from. We made a second pass and dropped our 750lbs bombs from above the clouds. Misty said we had stopped the convoy.

F-100D pilots had no night-flying technological aids or radar, and as Maj Don Schmenk recalled, "We relied on flares dropped by others. Everything that we dropped depended on the skill of the pilot. The aircraft had to arrive at the correct spot in space at the right dive angle, correct altitude and exact airspeed at the same time to ensure an accurate delivery."

Denying the darkness

Most troop and truck movements, or insurgent activity, occurred under the cover of darkness. To penetrate that camouflage briefly, flares were available for night attacks using techniques developed during *Farm Gate*. Also, flare shells were fired by artillery units. Banks of aircraft landing lights were installed in the open doorways of UH-1 helicopters to illuminate targets. Enemy troops inevitably fired at this searchlight display, but revealed their own positions to gunship helicopters lurking behind the "Lightning Bug" searchlight bearer. Some UH-1s had Nighthawk installations including an AN/VSS-3 xenon high-intensity searchlight which could also emit invisible infrared light. As a searchlight, it illuminated ground targets for strike aircraft but attracted antiaircraft fire. Nighthawk included an AN/TVS-4 night observation scope to work with the infrared searchlight and an XM-27E1 minigun system. These helicopters became successful in responding to troop movements revealed by ACOUSID sensors.

The PVS-2A Night Vision Sight for infantry use was another important innovation. Used by O-2A FACs, it provided many more targets for strike aircraft. In a three-day period in 1967, FACs, often using PVS-2As or AVG-3 Starlight scopes, detected 597 trucks, of which 83 were destroyed. In a similar period the previous year, the score was eight trucks destroyed. Night vision scopes could detect the shuttered headlights of trucks or even hand-held flashlights.

For longer-distance use over Laos, a few C-123 transport aircraft were fitted with banks of 28 high-intensity arc lights in their bellies. Orbiting at 12,000ft, they illuminated an area two miles in diameter but exposed themselves to 37mm AAA. The advent of AAA directed by SON-9 radars from 1969 required ECM protection by EB-66 Destroyers for flare-ships and some C-123 crews jury-rigged their own chaff dispensers. Other AN/AVG-3-equipped UC-123B/Ks of the 606th SOS at Nakhon Phanom, operating as "Candlesticks," provided both flare illumination and FAC duties over the *Barrel Roll* and northern *Steel Tiger* region with up to nine four-hour sorties per night. Blind Bat C-123s offered similar roles in southern *Steel Tiger*. Fifty flares (including red LUU-1Bs and infrequently used green LUU-5s based on Mk 24s, rather than 26 less bright Mk 6 "logs") could be launched off their cargo ramps, usually in threes so that an attack pilot could be orientated in relation to their three spots of light on the ground. Instructions such as "Bomb between the two northerly flares" were used rather than estimates in meters as the C-123 made left-hand orbits near the target. Working with "Big Eagle" A-26Ks, A-1s, and T-28s, they usually flew six-hour missions, providing valuable support for *Lam Son 719*. Aerial surveillance of the Trail and Blind Bats enabled Gen Westmoreland to anticipate the massive NVA assault on Khe Sanh.

RF-4 reconnaissance in *Barrel Roll*

RF-4C- 66-0396 "Bullwhip 1" of the 14th TRS, 432nd TRW at Udorn RTAFB, piloted by Capt C. P. Sloan and 1Lt A. L. Guise, is flying a post-strike dawn *Barrel Roll* photo reconnaissance mission over the Ho Chi Minh Trail 20 miles southeast of Ban Ban in northern Laos on December 21, 1969. Typically, they flew "straight-and-level" at around 3,500ft altitude at more than 500kt over jungle territory in early morning light. AAA gunners received warning of approaching aircraft from observers on the route. During this mission, the aircraft was hit by 37mm AAA and the crew ejected.

The 40 A-26Ks, refurbished by On-Mark Engineering for the 609th SOS, were camouflaged without national insignia. Crew members were "civilians" when flying over Laos, without identification cards and insignia. BLU-2 firebombs and two SUU-14 dispensers for CBU-14 were used to attack trucks. CBU-14 was replaced by CBU-25 in 1970 after a high failure rate. (USAF)

Of the F-4 squadrons that FACs called in, they found the 497th TFS Night Owls to be the most accurate night bombers, although USN and USMC A-4 Skyhawks often achieved the best daylight results against trucks. The Blind Bat mission was taken over by black-painted C-130As of the 374th Tactical Airlift Wing at Ubon from March 1966, teamed with "Yellowbird" B-57 bombers and USMC EF-10B ECM aircraft. They carried up to 350 Mk 24 marker parachute flares and 66 Mk 6 marker "logs" (visible as a white flame from 12,000ft, but sometimes extinguished with shovels of earth or replaced with decoy lights and fires by Trail workers) for strike and armed reconnaissance missions, delivered experimentally via a 14-round LAU-62 launcher above the C-130A's rear cargo ramp. Cheaper manual launching was reinstated after flares became jammed. Blind Bats often worked with O-2As to mark targets and used Starlight scopes fixed in the right rear paratroop door aperture during missions exceeding seven hours. The scope magnified the available light by 30,000 times. Blind Bats could also act as FACs for strike aircraft and illuminate targets for them, dropping up to four Mk 24 flares for each attack pass but attracting up to 300 rounds of AAA per sortie. Laser target markers for F-4 Pave Way I bombs were also tested in a Blind Bat C-130A.

Changing nature

Some of the more far-fetched scientific proposals failed in operational tests. One was Operation *Commando Lava*, begun in May 1967. C-130s dumped tons of a chemical solvent on mountain roads to turn soil into liquid mud in the rainy season, rendering tracks impassable. In response, Trail workers reinforced the soggy surface with rocks and branches. Project *Compatriot* from 1967 until July 1972 involved "cloud seeding" with silver iodide or lead iodide crystals in photoflash cartridges dispensed into cloud banks from Udorn-based WC-130 and RF-4C aircraft in the hope of releasing their moisture. Flooded tracks could halt traffic for a while and crops could be destroyed, but the effect of the seeding was usually uncertain.

Bombing could clear small areas of forest, using conventional bombs fused to explode above the ground. The massive 10,000lb BLU-82/B "Daisy Cutter" blast bomb, dropped from a CH-54 helicopter or a C-130 and exploding three feet above the ground, created a jungle landing zone 300ft in diameter with one blast. In addition to splintering trees, it could also collapse underground tunnels and bunkers, or explode whole fields of landmines. From 1967, CBU-55 fuel-air explosives (FAE) created and detonated an inflammable ethylene-oxide mist over a target area, producing over-pressure conditions 15 times greater than a conventional bomb and instantly clearing an area of forest 100ft in diameter.

More successful in the short term but devastating for the future of many of those affected by the projects, were the chemical defoliant programs to remove jungle cover. Chemical spraying missions using converted C-123 transport aircraft were approved by the JCS in January 1962. Training flights in Vietnam began in February and UC-123B 56-4370 became the first US aircraft to be lost in South Vietnam, crashing in dense forest near Bien Hoa and killing its three-man crew. Gradually, UC-123 aircraft equipped with spray-bars began to spray areas of Phuoc Long Province from October 1964. Each *Ranch Hand* UC-123 dispensed 950 gallons of Agent Orange, Agent Purple, Agent White (Tordon 101), or Agent Blue herbicides and defoliant over a ten-mile strip of land 230ft wide, killing crops, defoliating trees, and encouraging floods. Soon after the war, it became apparent that dioxin-laden Agent Orange caused birth defects in the children of those who had been exposed to it, including Americans, and would do so for many years.

The 11 venerable UC-123B/Ks of the Special Aerial Spray Flight *Ranch Hand*, 464th Troop Carrier Wing (TCW) at Da Nang had flown 19,000 sorties by 1968, spraying up to 1.5 million acres of forest and crops annually. During December 1965 alone, over 68,000 acres of crops and 253 square miles of forest were destroyed in 897 sorties. In May 1966, over 200,000 gallons of herbicide were sprayed and it was calculated that *Ranch Hand* was using up to 90 percent of US herbicidal chemical production. Flights were often canceled owing to shortages of chemicals. UC-123 numbers were increased to 19 and the aircraft were reassigned several times, first to the 315th TCW then to the 12th Air Commando Squadron, 315th Air Commando Wing at Bien Hoa AB in October 1966. In 1968, projects were in hand to defoliate half the area of South Vietnam, revealing incursion routes.

Many species of trees were still affected 40 years later, although bamboo growth recovered quite quickly. However, in an abrupt change of policy, crop destruction sorties were ended. Agent Orange, previously considered harmless to humans, was banned in 1970 and defoliation came to be regarded as unacceptable chemical and biological warfare. The last *Ranch Hand* sortie was flown on January 7, 1971, after nine years of operations in which eight UC-123s had been lost. An F-4 Phantom was equipped with a herbicide dispenser in one of its 370-gallon drop tanks in 1969 in the hope that the type would prove to be less vulnerable to ground fire than the ponderous UC-123, but the experiment was ended after an F-4 was shot down and a second lost its jury-rigged dispenser en route to a target.

Phantom IIs flew *Ranch Hand* escort sorties and a 390th TFS F-4C (63-7621) was hit by AAA on December 31, 1967, during a defoliation mission near Dak To. Maj Jake Sorensen and 1Lt "Mike" Aarni made high-speed passes each side of the UC-123s to deter the opposition but they were then asked to provide close air support with a FAC for a trapped Army unit. The two Phantoms each delivered six 750lb bombs, six 2.75in. rocket pods, and 20mm fire from SUU-16/A gun pods. On his final pass, Sorensen's aircraft took a hit in the belly. One engine flamed out and the other caught fire. The rocket motor of one of his four Sparrow missiles ignited but the missile remained in its well, accelerating the aircraft by 100kts. The remaining rounds in his gun pod then started to explode. With flames streaming 300ft behind the aircraft, the two men ejected and were recovered.

Another brief experiment with the twin-boom C-123 produced the AC-123K "Black Spot." Two (54-691 and 54-698) were equipped for night interdiction with a nose turret containing a laser rangefinder, a primary infrared sensor, LLLTV, radar for vehicle detection, and (in one example) a very effective S-Band "Black Crow" ignition detector. The sensors fed a computer which controlled 72 canisters containing up to 177 BLU-3 or BLU-26 bomblets. Released through SUU-24's 24 chutes, these munitions burst around trucks, ideally within 30 seconds of target detection by one of the sensors. "Black Spots" flew "Triton" missions with the 8th TFW in Laos during the period from December 1968 to May 1969 and were credited with 418 trucks, over half in first-pass attacks. Their need to operate below 5,000ft for target detection made them vulnerable to AAA, so for their second deployment in 1970 they had Zorro A-1 flak suppression escorts.

Forest fences

When the operational use of air-dropped sensors in Operation *Muscle Shoals* (renamed *Igloo White* in June 1968) began in September 1967, it was acknowledged that the slow-moving, low-flying VO-67 OP-2E sensor-dropping aircraft would be vulnerable to ground fire. The first loss occurred on January 11, 1968, a few weeks after their arrival at Nakhon Phanom RTAFB for *Commando Hunt* monitoring operations. In poor weather, OP-2E BuNo 131436 crashed into a 4,580ft mountain, killing its crew of nine. A second and its crew were lost on February 17, 1968. After the third loss, the squadron's *Igloo White* participation was reduced and minimum drop altitudes were raised to 5,000ft. That OP-2E, Bu No 131484, was hit by 37mm AAA as it "seeded" near the Ban Karai Pass and caught fire, filling the interior with toxic fumes. Seven crewmen bailed out and were rescued, but the aircraft commander, Cdr Paul Milius, remained aboard until they had all escaped. He bailed out at the last minute but was never found.

Many of the USN pilots flying the green OP-2Es had experience of dropping anti-submarine sonobuoys at around 500ft over the sea. Over Laos, they had to stay above 12,000ft to avoid AAA and then descend to treetop altitude, "jinking" all the way to avoid ground fire. When the target area for sensor-dropping was located, they climbed to 1,500ft, flying straight and level at 150–200kt to deliver the ACOUSIDs or ADSIDs, and then escaped at lower altitude before making a full-power climb to safer altitudes. Some aircraft had World War II Norden bombsights fitted to improve accuracy. The strenuous maneuvers needed at low altitude overtaxed these sedate patrol planes but they improved the chances of avoiding the numerous AAA weapons. At its operational altitude, the big OP-2E was a perfect target for 23mm and 37mm AAA gunners. Increasing ground-fire opposition forced them to drop from a slightly safer 3,000ft altitude and then to retreat to areas where there was less AAA.

VO-67 made its last sensor-drop on June 25, 1968, and it was deactivated on July 1 after making 260 drops, some of them during the relief of Khe Sanh. Col David Lownds, commanding the 26th Marines at Khe Sanh, was confident that the sensors had saved numerous lives, although the massive B-52 strikes were considered the main weapon for destroying enemy troop advances once they were detected. LORAN-equipped F-4D Phantom IIs of the 25th TFS then took over the sensor task, carrying pods which dispensed a string of 16 ADSIDs fairly accurately in a 550kt pass at altitudes below 1,500ft.

The ever-increasing small-arms and AAA fire in Laos forced two other propeller-driven strikers away from heavily defended areas in 1969. T-28 Trojans, operated by the Royal Laotian AF but often flown by USAF Raven Air Commando pilots, were among the earliest opponents to Pathet Lao aggression and movements along the Trail. They had been in action from South Vietnam within the terms of the Geneva Accords with the *Farm Gate* detachment of the 4400th CCTS (later, 1st Air Commando Squadron, Composite) since 1961 in a training capacity for the South Vietnamese Air Force, for whom it became the principal combat type until A-1 Skyraiders arrived in 1964. Many of these T-28D-5s (known locally as

F-28s) then passed to the 606th SOS at Nakhon Phanom where they flew missions over Laos, unmarked and camouflaged in green and black until 1972. Often, they had frames attached to their fuselages into which the national insignia of Thailand, Laos, or the USA could be inserted, depending on the political circumstances of the mission. Their ordnance loads of machine-gun pods, LAU-32A rocket pods, and Mk 81 bombs or SUU-14A CBU made them useful for low-level, pinpoint attacks in lightly defended areas. Easy to maintain, reliable, and maneuverable, the T-28 was a popular aircraft which proved that such simple types are valuable in a counter-insurgency war. It completed 3,876 missions between January 9, 1967, and USAF phase-out in 1968. Its "Zorro" call-sign was inherited by its replacement in the 56th SOW, the A-1.

OP-2E BuNo 131423/10 of VO-67 cruising over Laos on reciprocating engines only. The "MR" tailcodes derived from its initial tests in the Mud River area. (US Navy)

Bat Cats

Igloo White sensors were monitored by 553rd Reconnaissance Wing's refurbished ex-US Navy Lockheed EC-121R Super Constellations. After tests with a prototype in 1969, 30 of these former Air Defense Command aircraft were resurrected from the Davis-Monthan storage facility, converted, and camouflaged. Two-thirds had both active and passive ALT-27 and ALT-28 ECM equipment installed, as their missions occasionally took them over the North Vietnamese border where SAMs were a threat. All had the large radomes above and below the fuselage, used in their USN "Warning Star" radar reconnaissance days, removed by Lockheed. The "Connies" relied on four Wright R-3350-43 oil-leaking piston engines, which required intensive maintenance. Two flight engineers were included in the crew to keep the motors turning. Two aircraft were lost in accidents in 1969. 67-21493 was unable to take off successfully from Korat during a severe thunderstorm and crashed into trees with the loss of all 18 members of Crew 39. Bat Cat 19 (67-21495) hit approach lights on landing at Korat and crashed, killing four crew members. A third (67-21472) ran off the runway and crashed at Otis AFB, Massachusetts, but the rest survived their slow patrols over the Trails only to be scrapped at Davis-Monthan AFB in 1970–72.

After initial test flights at Korat in October 1967, the 533rd RW aircraft were fully operational by the end of the year with the 553rd and 554th RS. Missions consisted of

A 553rd RW EC-121R, call-sign "Bat Cat" (changed from "Ethan") on its *Igloo White* orbit over Laos at around 23,000ft. "Bat Cats" were also radio relay stations for aircraft flying over Cambodia. (USAF)

orbits at 14,000 to 18,000ft over Laos, Cambodia, South Vietnam, and the Gulf of Tonkin. Flights lasted from ten to 15 hours, extended to 18 hours by briefing and pre-flight duties, and flown at the rate of up to ten per crew each month. Each of the ten most common orbits was color-coded for a particular area. Bat Cats sometimes supported Army of Marines activity away from the Trails when US forces came under attack. Sensors were dropped around threatened outposts and Bat Cats monitored them, often providing data directly to ground commanders to help them direct their fire at enemy troops.

Each Bat Cat crew of 18 included eight Combat Information Monitors (CIM), supervised by a Combat Information Control Officer (CICO). CIMs could interrogate *Igloo White* sensors through 40 pre-assigned radio frequencies. They could listen in to transmissions from an acoustic sensor when it triggered one of their array of 27 small lights, each one linked to a sensor's electronic "address." Their data on movements was recorded on spreadsheets and passed to the CICO through headsets for entry on his plotting board. Tapes of North Vietnamese truck drivers chatting to each other, oblivious to the acoustic sensor above their heads, were played to members of Congress to demonstrate *Igloo White*'s value.

Electronic warfare officers (EWOs) were often aboard, increasing the crew total to 21. Crews were under threat from 37mm and radar-guided 57mm AAA guns, which could reach their operational altitudes. By 1969, they also faced, but escaped heavy 85mm and 100mm weapons. From 1971, Bat Cat operations were supported and eventually replaced by 33 manned or unmanned 553rd RW Pave Eagle I YQU-22A and Pave Eagle II QU-22B (Beech E-33 Debonair) piston-engine light aircraft, which provided low-cost, automatic radio-controlled relay stations for the sensor data. Operating from Nakhon Phanom RTAFB, they sustained seven combat losses and were considered fairly effective in duplicating the Bat Cat role, although their lower cost pleased the budget cutters in Washington. They lacked heating, de-icing and pressurization, causing an uncomfortable ride for a pilot, as one was usually carried. Two pilots were killed and there were several cases of engine failure.

The 553rd RS was deactivated on December 12, 1970, and it was merged with the 388th TFW. The last Bat Cat left on December 5, 1971, and modified C-130B transports took over the mission.

Gunships

During its initial operational trials in January 1965, the AC-47 gunship impressed commanders with its ability to beat enemy night attacks on US firebases. Night missions began on December 23, using the aircraft's load of 45 flares. An AC-47 forced Viet Cong to abandon an attack on a US special forces position at Tran Yen by deluging them with 4,500 rounds of ammunition. It then flew on to another US fort at Trung Hung and frustrated a similar Viet Cong attack. Sixteen of these missions were flown in December and a particularly successful four-hour attack on Viet Cong at Bong Song on February 8, 1965, using over 20,000 rounds, killed 300 troops. An attack on an exposed battalion near Nha Trang caused 400 enemy fatalities and in another an AC-47 crew fired 42,000 rounds.

The project's success led to a second AC-47 conversion in mid-1965, and three others temporarily equipped with less effective 0.30-cal guns. Eventually, 53 AC-47s were supplied. In February 1966, regular gunship and FAC Trail missions by four AC-47s began, although their main task was defending the perimeters of threatened US bases and outposts.

Using tactics practiced at Eglin AFB, AC-47 pilots circled to the left at 120kt around 3,000ft above a convoy, maintaining the correct angle and sighting the target with a grease-pencil mark on the cockpit window. The three gunners then opened up with their SUU-11/A gun pods, one in the aircraft's loading hatch and two from window apertures, saturating the targets with bullets at the rate of 18,000 rounds per minute. The pods housed GAU-2/A 7.62mm (0.30-cal) multi-barrel miniguns. An AC-47 unit, the 4th Air Commando Squadron (ACS), was established at Tan Son Nhut AB in Operation *Big Shoot* on November 14, 1965, with 20 aircraft. The 4th ACS moved to Nha Trang AB with the 14th Air Commando Wing (the so-called "Antique Wing" owing to its assortment of elderly, propeller-driven types) in May 1966 with a second squadron, the 3rd ACS. Both units were redesignated Special Operations Squadrons in August 1968 and they deployed flights to other bases, including Udorn, where AC-47s communicated directly with road-watch teams to be advised of targets. The gunship then dropped flares and attacked trucks or called in tactical strikes. Between December and July 1965, 243 trucks were claimed in this way.

Gunships quickly gained a reputation for preventing nocturnal assaults on US positions and intercepting troops on the Trail. They also participated in Operation *Niagara II*, the relief of Khe Sanh in January–April 1968. "Spooky"'s reliance on flares to illuminate targets revealed the aircraft to enemy gunners, and its lack of armor protection together with the three guns' short range made the aircraft vulnerable to enemy defenses. Twelve AC-47s were lost in action (mainly over South Vietnam) and seven to operational causes. Four were shot down in a six-month period,

The fabricated aluminum I-beam mount for the SUU-11A/1A minigun in the original AC-47 (0-48579 "Puff"), based on the experimental mounting used in C-131B 53-7820. The aircraft's "Puff the Magic Dragon" nickname was earned after a US Army reporter watched its fiery breath blasting Viet Cong attacking a fortified village. Guns were angled downwards by 12 degrees to reduce the aircraft's bank angle. (USAF)

AC-119G-FA "Shadow" 52-5927 of the 71st SOS, 14th SOW at Nha Trang AB. Despite having half of the AC-47's 4.5 hours' endurance, it was a stable gun platform for tackling base defense and protecting troops in contact with the enemy. (USAF)

General Electric/Emerson MXU-470 minigun modules in later AC-47Ds and AC-119s replaced the SUU-11/A gun pods. Ideally, "Spooky" pilots held a pylon turn accurately enough to place all gunfire within an area 150ft in diameter. The GAU-2/A gun fired 3,000 or 6,000 rounds per minute, usually in three-second bursts. (USAF)

three of them over Laos. Clearly, a more survivable "Gunship II" with heavier armament was required.

AC-119 "interim" gunships replaced AC-47s in the two "Spooky" units, beginning in December 1968 with a successful three-month evaluation. The AC-119G Shadows went to the 71st SOS, 14th SOW, at Nha Trang AB, flown mainly by USAF Reserve crews, while 12 Stingers were allocated to the 18th SOS, 14th SOW, from November 3, 1969. They were divided into flights which could be allocated to other airbases including Phan Rang, Da Nang, Nakhon Phanom, and Tan Son Nhut to provide local responses to enemy incursions. AC-119Gs and AC-47s shared the defense of Firebase Crook in Tay Ninh Province on June 7, 1969, killing 323 enemy troops.

The under-powered and less well-equipped AC-119Gs were as vulnerable to AAA as AC-47s, so they were confined mainly to operations over South Vietnam, while the more powerful, longer-ranging AC-119K Stingers could operate over the Trail. One Stinger destroyed a record 29 trucks in one mission over Laos. They could reach 5,500ft but customarily flew lower, using their somewhat unreliable fire control computers and night observation equipment to locate targets under jungle cover. The relatively short range of the 7.62mm gun pods required aircraft to remain below 2,000ft to concentrate their fire, putting them at severe risk from ground fire. Their 20mm guns also proved to be fairly ineffective against trucks and they often jammed. However, AC-119G crews had their own slogan: "When uninvited guests drop in, call for The Shadow. Who knows what evil lurks beneath the jungle canopy? The Shadow knows!"

Stingers confronted NVA tanks during Operation *Lam Son 719*, destroying eight PT-76 light tanks on February 28 with a single aircraft. The 71st SOS ended its operations in June 1969 and its aircraft were reallocated to the newly formed 17th SOS with regular USAF crews. After the US withdrawal from Vietnam, these gunships were donated to the SVAF's 819th and 821st squadrons, remaining in service until 1975. Despite their vulnerability, only five of these slow-moving killers were lost in action. Two were AC-119G operational losses attributed to the aircraft's limited takeoff power. Failure of one engine on takeoff caused an unrecoverable situation, a fate which befell AC-119G 52-5907 "Shadow 76" of Det.1, 17th SOS on October 11, 1969. An engine fire resulted in a crash which detonated its full load of ammunition and fuel, killing six of its crew of ten. The aircraft also proved to be capable of surviving severe damage. Capt Alan Milacek returned to Udorn on May 8, 1970, with an AC-119K that had 14ft of its wing and aileron blasted away by flak.

Spectre

After testing at Eglin AFB in the summer of 1967, the AC-130A prototype's initial ten-week perational test deployment was made from Nha Trang AB with Detachment 2 of the 14th SOW from September 21 in Project *Pave Pronto*. The AC-130A (which their crews liked to call "Fabulous Four Engine Fighters" after an unconfirmed 1969 shoot-down of a North Vietnamese helicopter) flew operational sorties over Laos and South Vietnam from September 27 and truck-busting flights began on November 8. During this test period, the AC-130A detected 94 trucks and destroyed 38 in South Vietnam and the *Tiger Hound* area.

A 16th SOS AC-130A at Ubon RTAFB in 1969. A Texas Instruments Moving Target Indicator and AN/AAD-4 Forward Looking Infrared (FLIR) were among its advanced equipment. Early AC-130A missions at 4,500ft and 145kt took around four hours and crews could expect to dodge about 500 rounds of AAA. (USAF)

A second visit attached to the 8th TFW at Ubon RTAFB began in February 1968 and 319 trucks were destroyed out of 847 detected.

In October 1968, the 16th SOS was organized at Ubon for the first four production AC-130As and they were allotted search areas of 20 by ten miles to patrol at 145kts and around 5,000ft using a variety of random search patterns rather than the AC-47's simple pylon turn. Three F-4D Phantom IIs, often 497th TFS "Night Owls," accompanied each Spectre night mission. Vital as escorts and flak suppressors, they cycled on and off a tanker aircraft, leaving an aircraft in place to deliver 2,000lb "Daisy Cutter" bombs or CBU-24 onto any AAA site that dared to fire at the AC-130. Phantom pilots monitored a Spectre's progress by following the shielded red anti-collision beacon on its upper fuselage. Pilots like Capt Gail Peck were amazed at the gunships' accuracy when they viewed the infrared imagery from its sensors after the mission. During the first half of 1969, they destroyed 2,105 trucks, averaging four per sortie.

Although their primary mission was truck-hunting, like other gunships the Spectres were employed to relieve embattled US Army positions, including one at Katum, where an AC-130 rained fire on VC guerrillas as they penetrated the camp's perimeter defenses. In many instances, ground commanders were prepared to call in the torrent of gunfire to positions very close to their own troops. No flak damage occurred until September 26, 1968, but the first of five losses happened on May 24, 1969. A 16th SOS AC-130A 54-1629 (call-sign "Carter") detected trucks on routes 914 and 920 near Ban Tanbok, and was about to fire at them from 6,500ft when it was hit in the tail section and right wing by two 37mm shells, damaging the elevator trim, rudder, and autopilot. The pilot, Lt Col Bill Schwehm with Spectre Crew Number One, managed to maintain limited control of the now massively tail-heavy AC-130 by using aileron trim and differential engine power. He coaxed the aircraft

16th SOS AC-130A 56-0490 "Thor," shot down by 37mm AAA on December 21, 1972, while truck-hunting. Radar emissions from the ground could interfere with the Black Crow ignition detector (left). A typical ammunition load was 15,500 rounds of 7.62mm and 8,000 rounds of 20mm. Firing the 20mm guns filled the aircraft with smoke temporarily. The 16th SOS squadron song was "Ghost Riders in the Sky." (USAF via Chris Hobson)

An ordnance crew manhandles the massive 105mm howitzer from a Pave Aegis AC-130E. Its recoil moved the gun backwards 44in. when fired, and required a compensating mechanism and a blast deflector to protect the left wing. It needed three gunners, trained by the US Army's 1st Cavalry Division. Each shot could be felt throughout the aircraft. (USAF)

back to Ubon. SSgt Troglen, the "vertical observer" operating a night-vision illuminator on the open tailgate, was fatally injured by the flak and the flight engineer died in the crash landing when the Hercules' previously damaged starboard landing gear failed to lock down. It ran off the runway, losing a wing when it hit the barrier cable structure.

Schwehm survived and nine crew members bailed out near the airfield. In their year of duty, his crew was credited with 228 trucks, with another 67 and a helicopter probably destroyed during 126 missions. Unsurprisingly, the AC-130 like the B-52 became a primary target for North Vietnam's gunners and their Soviet advisers.

The crew of AC-130A 54-1625 "The Warlord" claimed 56 trucks in March 1970 and another 18 on one mission in the Iron Triangle region on April 9 despite heavy flak. "The Warlord" as Adlib 01 was hit by 37mm fire during a *Commando Hunt* mission near Saravan, southern Laos on April 22, 1970, igniting the flares stored in its rear fuselage. It crashed in flames with the loss of ten of its 11 crew members. The pilot and three other crew members rode the aircraft into the ground to give the others a chance to escape. The following night, another 16th SOS Spectre and its 497th TFS Phantom II escort destroyed the offending 37mm gun sites.

Apart from a crash landing by AC-130A 55-0029 "Midnight Express" at Ubon, the big gunships survived their hazardous missions with few losses until the 1972 Easter Offensive brought far more AAA batteries onto the Trail, including mobile SAMs. All 14 crew members of 55-0044 "Prometheus" (which had been hit in 1971, losing both its starboard propellers)

Gunship interdiction over Laos

AC-130A 56-0490 "Thor," a Surprise Packet-equipped gunship, attacks three trucks on the Ho Chi Minh Trail near Pakse in southern Laos on December 21, 1972. The pilot, Capt Harry Lagerwall, fired his forward M61 20mm guns, but during his left-hand orbit, a 37mm shell hit the AC-130A at 7,500ft. Two of the 16 crew members bailed out. It was the final AC-130 loss of the war. "Thor" carried ANALQ-87 ECM pods because of the increased threat from SAMs in Laos. Under-wing SUU-42A/A chaff and flare ejector pods could also be carried. Heat deflectors shielded their engine exhausts to deter Strela missiles.

After Operation *Linebacker II*, B-52s maintained high sortie rates over northern Laos as North Vietnam sought to grab territory before the anticipated ceasefire. Truck parks and storage areas were destroyed, but after the ceasefire on February 22, 1973, Pathet Lao and NVA advances continued, so B-52 attacks were resumed. (USAF)

were killed when it was struck by an SA-2 on March 28 while hunting trucks near Khe Sanh. The pilot, Maj Irving Ramsower II, evaded the first two missiles in the salvo but the third blew the Hercules apart. By June of that year, a new weapon, the shoulder-launched, infrared SA-7 Strela, had been supplied to the NVA and it was used to bring down AC-130A 55-0043 near Hué. It homed onto the aircraft's No. 3 engine and a fuel tank exploded, blowing off the wing. Only three of the 15-man crew, which included some of the 16th SOS's most experienced flyers, escaped. The following night, another Strela was successfully decoyed away from an AC-130 by a hand-launched flare, and the missile's launch position was immediately hit by full bombloads from the 497th TFS Phantom escort. The final loss occurred on December 21, 1972. AC-130A 56-0490 "Thor" was shot down by 37mm at 7,500ft over the Ho Chi Minh Trail while attacking three trucks in southern Laos. As the fuselage gradually filled with leaking fuel, the gunship flew on towards Ubon, but the bail-out bell was not rung. Just before it finally caught fire and exploded, two of the 16 crewmen managed to bail out.

Increased AAA and SAM opposition meant upgraded countermeasures for AC-130s, with dual AN/ALQ-87 ECM pods to defeat the SAMs' Fan Song radars, additional chaff and flare dispensers, and improved armor protection. However, this did not prevent the only AC-130E loss, a Pave Aegis howitzer-carrier and the second Spectre casualty in two days. "Spectre 22" (69-6571) was engaging a group of trucks on the Trails near Muang Fandeng on March 30, 1972. Four were destroyed and the gunners were about to hit more as the aircraft circled at 7,500ft and 195kt. Several 57mm shells exploded on the right wing and fuselage, igniting an external fuel tank. The pilot, Capt Waylon Fulk, headed for Ubon but the damage was severe and all 15 crew members had to bail out near Saravan in southern Laos. A massive search and rescue operation ensued. Eight HH-53 helicopters were used, supported by 46 attack, ECM, gunship, and FAC aircraft, and Air America aircraft. Eleven flights of strike aircraft covered the rescue and seven of them attacked enemy forces. The entire AC-130E crew was rescued, including two who had landed 40 miles from the main group.

Even the A-1 Sandy aircraft operated by the 1st SOS in 1972 had to be equipped with modified flare pods to prevent SA-7s from homing onto their engine heat after three were lost to these missiles in mid-1972. Although an A-1 could dive at 400kt, its speed fell back to around 150kt in a climb away from a target, placing it at severe risk from all forms of AAA. Two A-1E/Gs were brought down by SA-7s during the same mission on May 1, 1972, while they searched for 1Lt William Seitz, whose A-1H fell victim to a Strela the previous day. All three pilots were rescued.

Lam Son 719

This major but final attempt to undermine the Trail took place from January 30, 1971, on Route 9 between Thailand and Vietnam. *Lam Son 719* was preceded by the US-led Operation *Dewey Canyon II* to clear Route 9 of mines and set up new firebases at Khe Sanh and other locations. Communist forces were prepared for an invasion of the South and they had imported large numbers of well-supplied troops to the area together with unexpected T-34 and T-54 tanks.

This influx led to one of the most spectacular successes on December 18, 1970. *Igloo White* sensors had registered the approach of a 12-truck convoy near Ban Bak, but the signals had stopped there and intelligence analysts guessed that they must have entered a truck park and supply dump. After confirmation of their location by a Covey FAC O-2A, a pair of F-4s made a night attack on the suspected site, causing over 6,500 secondary explosions that continued for ten days and extended over one square kilometer. Further strikes by 340 fighter sorties detonated massive explosions and destroyed 46 trucks in this major fuel and ammunition dump, despite frenetic opposition from hundreds of AAA weapons.

By 1971, the VNAF had taken over almost three-quarters of air combat operations but USAF FACs and airstrikes were still essential. For *Lam Son 719*, beginning on February 8, 1971, ARVN armored divisions with 16,000 troops in 34 battalions intended to advance into the southern Laotian panhandle, reach the already heavily bombed village of Tchepone, destroy enemy facilities, and then withdraw. The aim was to cut the Trail routes to Cambodia, forcing the North into a pitched battle if necessary. The ARVN advance, overseen by 20th TASS FACs, was delayed by weather and poor tactics, while US commanders seriously underestimated the local NVA strength. Tactical airpower was constrained by weather, although 1,358 B-52 sorties and extensive use of gunships caused considerable enemy losses. As ARVN troops approached Tchepone to encircle the North's battalions, the NVA, well briefed by spies, waited with heavy artillery, AAA, and tanks until 120 US helicopters arrived to deliver ARVN troops. They were met by some 300 AAA guns (70 of which were destroyed by Mk 84 LGBs) and even more machine-gun positions, together with SA-2 missiles. The four-phase campaign ended in April, with the withdrawal of all ARVN forces after suffering 35 percent losses and permanent damage to their morale and credibility as a fighting force to take over the defense of South Vietnam under President Nixon's "Vietnamization" policy without US troops on the ground.

Large quantities of NVA supplies were captured but the US lost 107 of 600 US helicopters and 79 US aviators. A massive air support effort, which comprised most of the limited success of the campaign, required 9,000 tactical sorties dropping 50,000 tons of bombs. The ARVN claimed over 13,000 enemy casualties (mostly from air attack) but their own military performance had been inadequate and had little effect on the Trail supply system. Although President Nixon declared the operation a success for Vietnamization, the political mood in Saigon began to turn against the USA. North Vietnamese and Pathet Lao advances into Laos accelerated but US air support for Vang Pao's forces steadily declined as US forces continued to leave Southeast Asia.

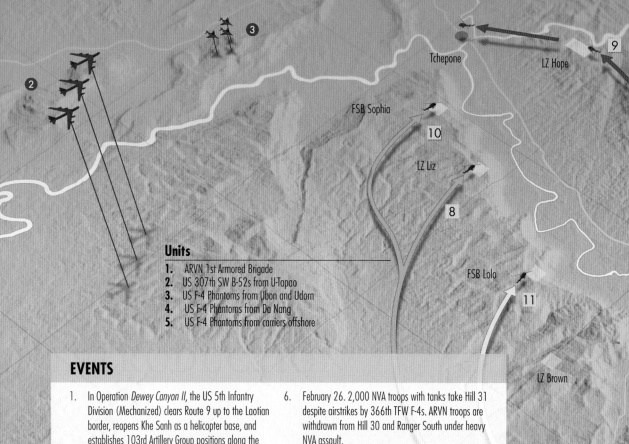

Units

1. ARVN 1st Armored Brigade
2. US 307th SW B-52s from U-Tapao
3. US F-4 Phantoms from Ubon and Udorn
4. US F-4 Phantoms from Da Nang
5. US F-4 Phantoms from carriers offshore

EVENTS

1. In Operation *Dewey Canyon II*, the US 5th Infantry Division (Mechanized) clears Route 9 up to the Laotian border, reopens Khe Sanh as a helicopter base, and establishes 103rd Artillery Group positions along the Laotian border. The 101st Airborne Division makes a feint attack towards the A Shau Valley.

2. February 8. The ARVN 1st Armored Brigade moves into Laos on Route 9 expecting to take Tchepone in three days. B-52s strike the proposed landing zones (LZs) and AAA positions along Route 9 and "Daisy Cutter" bombs are dropped to clear forest LZs and NVA troop concentrations. The 48th Assault Helicopter company moves to LZ Hotel to airlift troops. 100 tactical strikes are flown.

3. The ARVN 1st Infantry Division is helicoptered to LZ Delta by 158th Aviation Battalion and 223rd Combat Aviation Battalion UH-1C/Ds supported by AH-1Gs and fighters. The ARVN 1st Airborne Division and 1st Ranger Group are helicoptered to LZs Ranger North, Ranger South, and Hills 30 and 31.

4. February 10. Poor road surfaces halt the 1st Armored Brigade at Aloui. It is joined by the 9th Airborne Battalion. The NVA moves 37mm AAA into the area and lines the mountain sides around Route 9 with 14.5mm and 12.7mm guns. By February 11, 16,000 ARVN troops have been helicoptered in.

5. February 20. NVA forces take Ranger North despite tactical airstrikes, and a helicopter extraction is attempted on February 21. B-52 strikes are increased to 1,200 per month.

6. February 26. 2,000 NVA troops with tanks take Hill 31 despite airstrikes by 366th TFW F-4s. ARVN troops are withdrawn from Hill 30 and Ranger South under heavy NVA assault.

7. March 3. 3/1st ARVN Infantry Regiment is helicoptered to LZ Lolo after the area is "prepped" by B-52s and smokescreens are laid by fighters. Amid heavy opposition, seven helicopters are shot down. B-52s bomb within 300ft of ARVN occupants. Enemy attacks on other firebases are stopped by CAS.

8. March 4/5. ARVN forces helicoptered to LZs Liz and Sophia after preparatory airstrikes.

9. March 6. The ARVN 2nd Infantry Regiment is helicoptered to LZ Hope. B-52s bomb area around Tchepone and ARVN forces take and destroy the village and many supply dumps there.

10. March 11/12. ARVN forces are withdrawn from LZs Sophia and Liz.

11. March 16. Three ARVN battalions at LZ Lolo withdraw on foot but the 4th Battalion remains and is engaged by NVA troops. After intense fighting and airstrikes, only 36 survivors can be helicoptered out.

12. March 19 to April 6. The 1st Armored Division attempts to retreat along Route 9 but comes under heavy NVA attack and is frequently halted. The 17 damaged tanks it was towing are abandoned and destroyed by AH-1G gunships. LZ Hotel is abandoned. The campaign is ended on April 6. NVA use of the Trail increased.

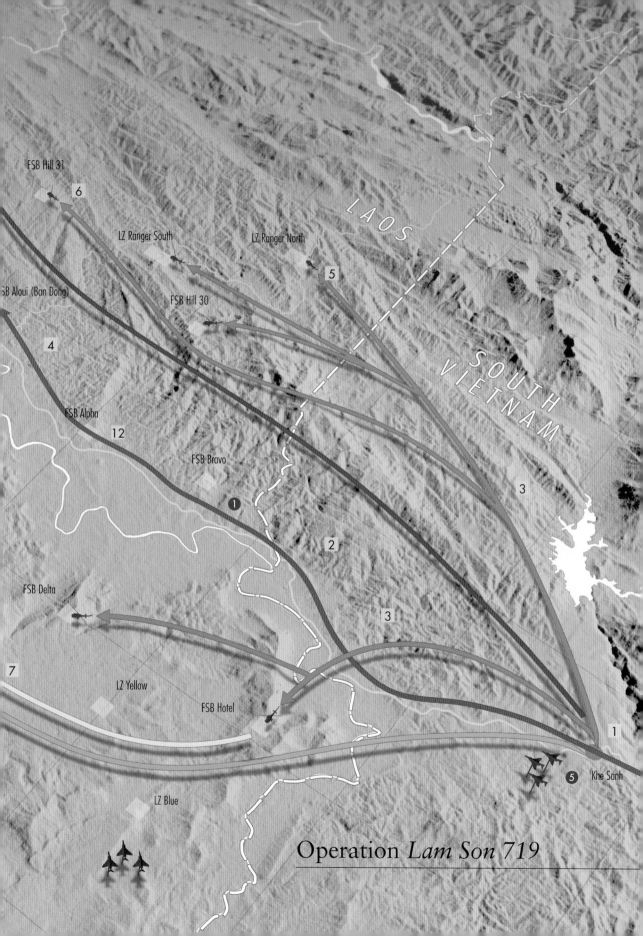

FSB Hill 31

6

LZ Ranger South

LZ Ranger North

5

FSB Aloui (Ban Dong)

FSB Hill 30

4

FSB Alpha

12

FSB Bravo

1

2

FSB Delta

3

3

7

LZ Yellow

FSB Hotel

1

LZ Blue

5 Khe Sanh

LAOS

SOUTH
VIETNAM

Operation *Lam Son 719*

AFTERMATH AND ANALYSIS

A welcome sight for any shot-down aviator. A 40th ARRS HH-53 hauls a pilot aboard but exposes itself to ground fire, demanding intensive suppression by "Sandy" A-1s. An epic six-hour battle in Laos to rescue the 60 troops and crew from two downed CH-53 helicopters on October 6, 1969, kept six 602nd SOS Sandy aircraft on station against surrounding enemy troops. (USAF)

Operation *Rolling Thunder* could not destroy North Vietnam's war-making capability, since the vast majority of its munitions, fuel, and training were resupplied by foreign nations. As the ports and rail centers receiving those supplies were "off limits" for attack, the campaign to block the Trail was America's main hope of diminishing the North's ambitions. The impossibility of eliminating more than a proportion of that supply network was undoubtedly one of the main reasons Hanoi was never forced into capitulation or even a lasting peace agreement.

In 1965, Admiral Ulysses S. Grant Sharp Jr advocated airpower as the means of cutting the lines of communication between North and South Vietnam through Laos by interdicting the Trail in the panhandle region. Constant attacks on choke points and bridges by day and night would, in his estimation, defeat Hanoi's attempts to occupy the South. During the early years of the subsequent campaign, not much more than 30 percent of the traffic was destroyed. Troop casualties probably averaged around 25 percent but many were due to disease and desertion rather than air action. The vastness of the area, the impenetrability of the forest, and the weather and the limited numbers of available aircraft all prevented that total from increasing significantly despite the assistance of highly sophisticated technology. The Trail campaign was proof for many analysts that wars cannot be won by airpower alone, particularly when bombing pauses allow the enemy to increase his defenses and infrastructure unimpeded.

Although the supply routes were never closed, the various efforts by US forces undoubtedly reduced the flow and, at times, destroyed up to a half of the materiel en route. This was the most that the US government could realistically expect of the campaign. The cost to those who transported the goods was high, with over two deaths of Trail travelers and three trucks for every hundred tons of supplies successfully delivered, roughly a day's deliveries in 1965. However, only 60 tons (20 truckloads) per day were usually needed to sustain insurgent activities in the South.

In crude economic terms, programs like *Igloo White* were hardly cost-effective. With annual running costs of $1 billion, it was estimated that each truck successfully tracked and destroyed cost the USA $100,000. AC-130 crews claimed 7.34 trucks destroyed per sortie in

1970 and 6,000 trucks destroyed in 1971; 89 percent of those attacked. USAF estimates of trucks destroyed in *Commando Hunt* were increasingly challenged from 1969 onwards, when the CIA figure of 6,000 trucks on strength in North Vietnam was compared with a claim of 12,368 destroyed in 1970. It was a war in which exaggerated statistics of success in terms of missions flown, ordnance dropped, and targets (real or theoretical) destroyed were grist to the mill of political vote-catching and career advancement for the "rear echelon" war managers.

In *Commando Hunt V* in 1971–72, Saigon analysts revised the USAF's claim for 16,266 trucks down to 11,000 destroyed – a figure which clashed with Hanoi's claim that only another 6,000 vehicles were received in 1972. The official weekly average of trucks destroyed by all gunships in their 2,400 sorties in *Commando Hunt V* was 65. The 62,100 tactical fighter sorties at that time claimed 579 trucks and storage areas weekly (the two types of target were combined in official statistics, but trucks were in the majority).

By 1970, intelligence gleaned from *Igloo White* and MACV-SOG generated precise locations, accurate to within 300ft, of 59 truck parks on the network. Although this knowledge enabled strike forces to destroy a higher proportion of the daily traffic (a figure of roughly two-thirds was claimed in 1970), the North Vietnamese compensated for this expected attrition by sending far more goods southwards than they would need. They also had large numbers of trucks in reserve in North Vietnam, immune to American bombing, enabling them to keep up to between 500 and 1,000 on the Trail on any night of the dry season from 1970.

The intelligence network used for the *Igloo White* program relied on comparatively early computer technology, which was just beginning to yield consistently useful results in the final years of the war. For much of the operation, the time lag between receiving sensor data at Nakhon Phanom and attacking a suspected target was up to six hours, giving enemy forces time to escape. Usually, delays were caused by the time taken to receive permission to attack from authorities in Saigon and Vientiane. Also, the volume of traffic in 1967–68 greatly exceeded the number of strike sorties that could be generated. At times many vehicles drove

Pilatus Porter N360F reached Air America in June 1967. It took ground fire several times, experienced a runway collision that tore off its left wing, rudder, and tailplane, and crashed in October 1970 after engine failure, ripping off both wings and the engine. Repaired and returned to service after both accidents, it was eventually abandoned at Tan Son Nhut AB in 1975. (Ken Marshall via Neil Aird)

Delivered to the USAAF in October 1944, this aircraft became an AC-47D with the 4th ACS/SOS. Hit in the mid-fuselage by small-arms fire at night on January 8, 1967, it crashed in flames, killing the crew of seven. (USAF)

through southern Laos with their headlights on, confident that their numbers reduced the chances of aerial attack.

The *Igloo White* system detected many of them, too, but follow-up strikes were inadequate. In the four months from December 1, 1967, 4,665 possible targets were identified but only 12 percent could be verified by aircrew and only half of those were attacked. In all, 569 aircraft received *Igloo White* data to instigate attacks during that time but only 282 attacks were actually carried out, destroying an estimated 384 trucks. By any calculations, picking off trucks one at a time on the Trail rather than hitting the long convoys that waited in North Vietnam to cross into Laos, or the shiploads of trucks being offloaded regularly at Haiphong docks, was inevitably massively wasteful and inefficient. As for pedestrian traffic, the difficulty of distinguishing troop movements from those of innocent civilians by using sensors alone could well have cost many lives.

Igloo White has influenced military command and control systems ever since. The addition of satellite reconnaissance, sideways-looking radar, and more sophisticated ground sensors has made the task of detecting, tracking, and attacking covert enemy forces more feasible, albeit at even greater expense.

Much of the ordnance aimed at the Trail came from B-52s flying 23,000 sorties over Laos between 1969 and 1971. Although the bombing of North Vietnam was the most publicized aspect of the Vietnam air war, it received less than one tenth of the total bomb tonnage dropped on Southeast Asia during that war.

As in all wars, truth was a major casualty in the Vietnam conflict. US pilots often heard rumors that North Vietnamese antiaircraft gunners and truck drivers were chained to their seats. North Vietnamese troops traveling south were assured that their grueling Trail journey would end in a warm welcome as liberators by the majority of the South Vietnamese

population. For the USA the impossibility of ascertaining the true fate of its lost pilots within the terms of the Geneva Convention persisted throughout the campaign. The standard practice in many parts of Laos was to execute such pilots unless North Vietnamese troops got there first and took them off to prison. When the Peace Accords led to a release of US prisoners from Hanoi only ten were listed as having been captured in Laos out of 333 who were known to have been lost there and information on others was not revealed.

General Westmoreland's HQ reported that in 1967–68, "the emphasis changed from nominating a maximum number of new target candidates to a broader intelligence role of nominating only the most lucrative targets such as large convoys." More energy was also devoted to monitoring choke points, road cuts, and blockages caused by bombing. Attacking road transport seemed to be a more profitable approach than attempting to intercept personnel en route, partly because of the lack of effective CBU weapons in 1967. MACV estimates of the numbers of troops infiltrating South Vietnam along the Trails show 6,700 in January 1967, rising to a peak of 33,000 in March 1968, bringing the total within the South and Laos to 117,165 personnel. 1968 saw by far the biggest influx ahead of the Tet Offensive, with 131,000 troops making the journey compared with 45,200 the previous year. It also saw the most intensive air activity over the Trail, with aircraft from all three US services, the CIA, the Laotian Air Force, and the Royal Australian Air Force in constant action. In 1971, the attacks on the Trail network aimed to prevent another Tet-type assault on the South.

The Helio U-10B Courier 63-13093 of the 5th SOS in January 1969. U-10s were among the most useful utility light aircraft for the Laos campaign, used extensively by Air Commando squadrons for resupplying "Lima" sites in Laos. (USAF)

Reconnaissance photos showed whether the previous night's strikes had damaged or destroyed trucks. Ahead of the Tet Offensive in 1968, FACs were regularly reporting up to 250 trucks per night, almost ten times as many as in the previous year. (USAF)

One of the most important aspects of the Trails war was the rapid development of innovative military technology to face the unexpected challenges it posed. Development of effective night-attack methods was crucial. In 1966, only 10 percent of USAF sorties in Laos and South Vietnam were flown at night, while 80 percent of Trail vehicular traffic moved in darkness. The *Shed Light* project gradually found some far-reaching solutions.

Among the most effective innovations was the gunship concept, particularly the AC-130. The aircraft's advanced sensors and devastatingly accurate armament made it one of the most feared weapons in the US armory. When President Nixon awarded the Presidential Unit Citation to the 16th SOS in May 1970 (an unusual award for a single squadron with only six aircraft), it was for the destruction of 1,300 trucks and damage to another 560 in 580 missions. However, the AC-130's slow on-target speed and low operational altitude made it vulnerable to ground fire. Its armament could obliterate targets effectively and often caused spectacular secondary explosions when ammunition trucks or dumps were hit, but trucks could sometimes survive gunfire damage without catching fire if they carried other types of load. AC-130s remained in service for over 30 years and they were vital weapons in the conflicts in Iraq in the 1990s, and more recently in Afghanistan. In 2017, the AC-130J Ghostrider entered service and the USAF expects to operate 37 of these upgraded versions by 2023.

The introduction of laser-guided munitions came comparatively late in the war. Their accuracy in taking out pinpoint targets in North Vietnam in 1972 was echoed in the Trail war too. Defense Research Deputy Director Leonard Sullivan estimated that the efficiency of an F-4 LGB team with 2,000lb bombs reduced the need for sorties to cut a section of the Trail by 80 percent. Their success against 57mm AAA gun sites, always a tough target, was also noted and PACAF analysts calculated that 10 percent of the AAA guns on the Trail were neutralized by "smart" bombs.

In 1967, scientists developed battery-powered camouflage detectors, binoculars with filters that could distinguish cloth and camouflage paint from natural growth, revealing troops and guns beneath camouflage netting from 10,000ft. Small numbers were issued to O-2A FAC pilots and they were used very effectively over southern Laos until 1972.

At the other extreme of the technological spectrum, simple and reciprocating engine types like the T-28 Trojan, A-26K, and A-1 Skyraider were vital weapons throughout the war. Their heavy ordnance loads and ability to fly slowly at low level enabled them to identify and attack targets that were inaccessible to fast-moving jets. It was estimated that one A-26K "Nimrod" sortie could cover the same target area as six jet fighters with much shorter endurance. That lesson still influences the USAF today in its choices for its Light Attack Aircraft program.

Despite America's overall technical superiority, there were still occasions when its forces were unprepared for innovations by the enemy. The Soviet SA-7 Strela infrared homing missile was known to the West, but its combat debut during the 1972 Easter Offensive caught AC-130 crews off guard. Several A-1, OV-10A, and O-2A aircraft (in which the rear engine was particularly vulnerable to IR missiles) had already fallen to the small, deadly missile forcing FACs to adopt a 7,000ft minimum altitude. Three O-2As and an O-1 were lost on May 11 and 14, 1972, three of them to Strelas. An AC-130 was attacked on May 12 and a crewman saw four SA-7s heading for his aircraft. A fifth approached unseen from below the Hercules, homing onto the infrared 2kW Xenon searchlight which an operator was holding out over the aircraft's open tailgate. The missile exploded inside

The first deliveries of the O-2A "Oscar Duck" went to the 20th Tactical Air Support Squadron at Da Nang AB on July 2, 1967, with "Big" call-signs. Its fore-and-aft "suck and blow" engines made it faster than the Cessna O-1 but its disadvantage for FACs was side-by-side seating, restricting the pilot's view to the right and allowing exit only from the right side. Extra transparencies were added but omitted from black-painted, night-operating O-2s. (USAF)

The AC-130's FLIR system, mounted in the wheel-well fairing, detected truck-sized objects from 20,000ft, tracking them even under tree cover. The AN/AWG-13 computer linked all the sensors and guns, so the pilot only had to aim his gunsight "pipper" at a target (at specific speeds and altitudes) and fire. (USAF)

the fuselage, injuring the operator and causing severe shrapnel damage inside the aircraft. Fortunately, the pilot was able to return to Ubon.

The Trail war continued after the Paris Peace Accords ended hostilities with North Vietnam on January 27, 1973. Electronic intelligence flights by veteran Douglas EC-47s were conducted until May 14, 1974, and an EC-57Q Radio Direction Finding version (43-48636) of the 361 TWES, 56 SOW at Ubon RTAFB was shot down near Saravan in southern Laos while tracking tanks heading south along the Trail on February 4, 1973. All eight crew members were killed.

The final invasion of the South, known as the Ho Chi Minh Campaign, began on April 26, 1975, when enough of the Trail network had been improved for heavy military traffic to reach Saigon. USAF gunships remained in action, covering the evacuation of Saigon in Operation *Frequent Wind* and the withdrawal from Phnom Penh in Operation *Eagle Pull*. After that, they patrolled the Thai border and identified NVA sapper groups that were trying to enter the country. Thai Army forces then closed in and killed the insurgents. One of their final acts was to cover the attempt to rescue the crew of the US merchant ship *Mayaguez* in May 1975, after it had been seized by Cambodia. Gunships also assisted the USMC withdrawal from Koh Tang Island after their unsuccessful rescue attempt for the crew. AC-130s sank several Khmer Rouge gunboats during this brief action.

Postwar, one of the most lasting legacies for Laos was the vast quantity of unexploded ordnance (UXO) in the Trails areas. Out of the millions of weapons dropped, including 1,150,000 tons of bombs, it was inevitable that a proportion would be wrongly fused, faulty, or incorrectly delivered. Local people in search of profit from the metal were often killed by exploding bombs. At best, the ordnance was used in ingenious ways in constructing buildings. Thousands of fuel drop tanks became boats, cladding for houses, or valuable scrap metal. In 2020, defusing the UXO is still a huge international operation, mainly to facilitate mineral exploration and logging in Laos. The death toll from as yet undiscovered bombs and the long-term effects of chemical deforestation will continue far into the future.

FURTHER READING

Appy, Christian G., *Vietnam*, Ebury Press, London (2003)

Bell, Don and the Tiger FACs, *The Tiger FACs*, Outskirts Press, Denver, Colorado (2014)

Berry, F. Clifton Jr, *Gadget Warfare*, Bantam Books, Toronto (1987)

Burns, David M., *Spectre Gunner*, iUniverse, Bloomington, Indiana (2013)

Churchill, Jan, *Hit My Smoke! Forward Air Controllers in Southeast Asia*, Sunflower University Press, Manhattan, Kansas (1997)

Conboy, K. and Bowra, K., *The NVA and Viet Cong*, Osprey Publishing, Oxford (1992)

Conboy, K. and Bowra, K., *The War in Cambodia 1970–75*, Osprey Publishing, Oxford (1989)

Conboy, K. and Bowra, K., *The War in Laos*, Osprey Publishing, Oxford (1989)

Davis, Larry, *Gunships*, Squadron Signal Publications, Carrollton, Texas (1982)

Diller, Richard E., *Firefly: A Skyraider's Story*, Dog Ear Publishing, Indianapolis (2013)

Drury, Richard S., *My Secret War*, Aero Publishers, Inc., Fallbrook, California (1979)

Fitzgerald, Frances, *Fire in the Lake*, Little, Brown and Company, New York (1972)

Gilster, Herman L., *The Air War in Southeast Asia: Case Studies of Selected Campaigns*, University Press of the Pacific, Honolulu, Hawaii (2002)

Harrison, Marshall, *A Lonely Kind of War: Forward Air Controller, Vietnam*, Presidio Press, New York (1989)

Lanning, Michael Lee and Cragg, Dan, *Inside the VC and the NVA*, Texas A&M University Press, Austin, Texas (2008)

Marrett, George J., *Cheating Death: Combat Air Rescues in Vietnam and Laos*, Smithsonian Books, Washington, DC (2003)

Mikesh, Robert C., *B-57 Canberra at War 1964–1972*, Ian Allan, Shepperton, UK (1980)

Morris, Virginia and Hills, Clive, *A History of the Ho Chi Minh Trail: The Road to Freedom*, Orchid Press, Bangkok (2006)

Newman, Rick and Shepperd, Don, *Bury Us Upside Down: The Misty Pilots and the Secret Battle for the Ho Chi Minh Trail*, Presidio Press, New York (2006)

Parker, James E., *Covert Ops: The CIA's Secret War in Laos*, St. Martin's Press, New York (1995)

Peck, Gaillard R. Jr, *Sherman Lead: Flying the F-4D Phantom II in Vietnam*, Osprey Publishing, Oxford (2019)

Prados, John, *The Blood Road: The Ho Chi Minh Trail and the Vietnam War*, John Wiley and Sons, Inc., Hoboken, New Jersey (1998)

Pribbenow, Merle L., *Victory in Vietnam: The Official History of the People's Army of Vietnam, 1954–75*, University Press of Kansas, Lawrence, Kansas (2002)

Robbins, Christopher, *The Ravens: Pilots of the Secret War in Laos*, Transworld Publishers, London (1988)

Rottman, Gordon L., *US MACV-SOG Reconnaissance Team in Vietnam*, Osprey Publishing, Oxford (2011)

Shepperd, Don, *Misty: First Person Stories of the F-100 Fast FACs in the Vietnam War*, 1st Books (2002)

Sikora, Jack and Westin, Larry, *Batcats*, iUniverse, Inc., Lincoln, Nebraska (2003)

Tang, Truong Nhu, *A Vietcong Memoir*, Vintage Books, New York (1985)

Whitcomb, Darrel D., *The Rescue of Bat 21*, Naval Institute Press, Annapolis, Maryland (1998)

Wood, Richard, *Call Sign Rustic: The Secret Air War Over Cambodia, 1970–73,* Smithsonian Institute Press, Washington, DC (2002)

Yarborough, Tom, *Da Nang Diary: A Forward Air Controller's Gunsight View of Flying with SOG,* Casemate Publishers, Philadelphia, and Oxford (2013)

Documents and Official Histories

Anthony, V. B., *Tactics and Techniques of Night Operations, 1961–1970,* Office of Air Force History, Washington, DC (March 1973)

Banner, Gregory T., *The War for the Ho Chi Minh Trail,* Thesis at the Faculty of the US Army Command and General Staff College (1979)

Hartsook, Dr Elizabeth and Slade, Stuart, *Air War Vietnam Part II – Plans and Operations 1969–75,* Defense Lion Publications (2012)

Nalty, Bernard C., *Air War Over South Vietnam, 1968–1975,* Air Force History and Museums Program, Washington, DC (2000)

Nalty, Bernard C., *The War Against Trucks: Aerial Interdiction in Southern Laos,* Air Force History and Museums Program, Washington, DC (2005)

Pfau, Richard A. and Greenhalgh, William H., *The B-57G Tropic Moon III 1967–1972,* Office of Air Force History, HQ USAF (1978)

Rowley, Ralph A., *Forward Air Control in Southeast Asia 1961–64,* Office of Air Force History, Washington, DC (1972)

Schlight, John, *The War in South Vietnam: The Years of the Offensive 1965–1968,* Office of Air Force History, Washington, DC (1988)

Van Staaveren, Jacob van, Wolk, Herman S., and Slade, Stuart, *Air War Vietnam. Plans and Operations 1961–1968,* Defense Lion Publications (2013)

Van Staaveren, Jacob, *Interdiction in Southern Laos 1960–1968,* Center for Air Force History, Washington, DC (1993)

INDEX